FROM CONFUCIUS TO CHRIST

DR. PAUL K. T. SIH

Dr. Sih broadcasting over United Nations Radio
Courtesy of the United Nations

FROM CONFUCIUS

TO CHRIST

BY

PAUL K. T. SIH

Professor and Director
Institute of Far Eastern Studies
Seton Hall University, New Jersey

SHEED & WARD, INC. NEW YORK, 1952

MANUFACTURED IN THE UNITED STATES OF AMERICA

TO

MARY IMMACULATE

MOTHER OF DIVINE GRACE
THE FIRST CONFESSION OF MY FAITH
IS DEDICATED
WITH FILIAL GRATITUDE
AND IN PRAYERFUL HOPE THAT
SHE
MAY OFFER US TO HER SON
AS CAPTIVES OF DIVINE LOVE

ACKNOWLEDGEMENTS

The author wishes to express his sincere appreciation to the following for their kindly and valuable assistance in the writing of this book:

To His Excellency Most Reverend Fulton J. Sheen, Auxiliary Bishop of New York, for his courteous generosity in taking time in a particularly busy period to write the preface.

To Father Thomas O'Melia, Father John J. Considine, and Mr. Frank Sheed, for their assistance and practical advice all along the way.

To His Excellency Most Reverend Raymond A. Lane, Superior General of Maryknoll, Right Reverend Monsignor John M. McNulty, President of Seton Hall University, and Father John J. Cain, Regent of the Institute of Far Eastern Studies, Seton Hall University, without whose generous encouragement this book might never have appeared.

To His Excellency Most Reverend Joseph M. Gilmore, Bishop of Helena, Montana, Reverend Mother

Acknowledgements

du Sacré Coeur Smith, R.S.H.M., Dean of Marymount College, Father Joseph S. McGrath of the University of Portland, Father John J. McCarthy, Father John T. S. Mao, Father Paul Chen, and Dr. N. J. Wu, for their continued counsel and interest.

To Miss Ruth Reidy, without whose help the author would have been more than normally helpless.

To Miss Mary Alice Ping and Miss Miriam F. O'Donnell for their assistance in reading the manuscript and checking references and footnotes.

PREFACE

In the Annals of the Celestial Empire, there is historical evidence of Ambassadors having been sent toward the West in search of "the great saint who was to appear." The following from the *Annals* narrates the circumstance:—"In the twenty-fourth year of the Tchao-Wang, of the dynasty of the Tcheou, on the eighth day of the fourth moon, a light appeared in the southwest which illuminated the King's palace. The monarch, struck by its splendor, interrogated the sages, who were skilled in foretelling future events. They then showed him books in which it was written that this prodigy signified the appearance of a great saint in the west, whose religion was to be introduced into this country. The King consulted the ancient books, and having found the passages corresponding with the time of Tchao-Wang, was filled with joy. Then he sent the officers Tsa-Yu and Thsin-King, the learned Wang-Tsun and fifteen other men to the West to obtain information." So sensible were these wise men of the time and place of the Savior's birth that they set forth to hail the expected Redeemer. The envoy encountered on the way the missionaries of Buddhism coming from India announcing an Incarnate God; these the Chinese took for the disciples of the true Christ, embraced their teaching, and introduced them to their fellow countrymen as the teachers of the true religion. Thus was Buddhism introduced into China in place of Christianity.

China had two other great chances to become Christian—one in the Middle Ages, the other at the close of the Ming Dynasty. Whether or not these were instances of rejected grace must be hidden in the councils of God. It is a fact that now China is beginning to have the dim beginnings of Faith—one percent of its four hundred fifty million people already embracing the Faith. Deeper than all political and economic crises of the present, is the apocalyptic fact that the day is dawning when the East will receive the gift of Faith, and when the Christ Who has been wounded and crucified in the Western world, will go to the East for the healing of His wounds. Communism is only an interlude in the shifting and transformation of world power from the West to the East. As one Communist officer recently put it: "It may be that all we are doing in China is preparing the way for the Catholic Church." Communism is the manure of civilization, the death which is spread upon the fields in the winter of discontent as a harbinger for the fruits and herbs of a rich and beautiful springtime.

The story of Dr. Paul K. T. Sih narrated in these pages is more than the story of an Oriental who has found Christ; it is rather a symbol of the leaven which is already working within the soul of China itself.

Three considerations emerge from this spiritual autobiography. First, how much the great philosophers of the East prepare for the Church. What Plato was to Augustine and Bonaventure, what Aristotle was to Aquinas, that the ethical philosophers of the East are to those destined to receive the grace of God: natural stepping-stones to the supernatural edifice of the Church. How very wrong it is for a missionary to feel that he must completely disabuse the Eastern minds of their great traditions before giving them even the beginnings of Christianity. Without knowing it, the Eastern peoples in their love of Confucius, Buddha, Mencius and others, were actually thinking about what Saint Paul told the Athenians, was the "unknown God." Dr. Wu, who helped lead Dr. Sih, his compatriot, to the Church, once said that Confucius led him to Christ. One derives the impression from this work of Dr. Sih that all the wise men of China helped prepare him, as much as nature can prepare anyone, for the gift of Faith. As St. Thomas said, "Nature inclines us to love God, its author, more than ourselves." In this connection, one is very much touched by the devotion to Küan-yin, the Chinese Goddess of Mercy. It is said that at her death, rather than surrender her virginity, she went to hell. She so diffused mercy and love through hell that the devil ordered her to leave. She is now on earth according to the Chinese tradition, and will not go to heaven until the very last soul is saved. As Dr. Sih puts it, "Last but not least, the popular Buddhist prayer, 'Küan-yin, Goddess of Mercy, save the poor and the hapless in the glory of Buddha,' was a solid mental foundation that enabled me to say very naturally the Angelic Salutation: 'Hail Mary, full of grace, the Lord is with Thee.' "

The second interesting fact that emerges from this autobiography is that when an Oriental is converted, he never turns back upon his natural culture, but with gratitude towards its natural foundations, seeks to supernaturalize them with his newly acquired gift of Faith. As the Chinese proverb has it, "When you drink the water, you must think gratefully of its source." As a man thinks more highly of his body when he more totally dedicates his soul to God, so too does a convert from Eastern philosophy think more highly of it, once he has embraced the Saviour of the world. It is interesting to note at this point how very much Communism demands fitting one's mind, culture, education, press into the mind of Moscow and yet how much when a man surrenders himself to Christ his country, its art, its family life, its government all begin to acquire a new emergence in freedom and in dignity. As Matthew the publican was a betrayer of the best interests of Israel when he was at receipt of customs, and then became the greatest of all the patriots of Israel quoting their prophets ninety-nine times in his gospel, after he had found Christ, so now Dr. Sih does not disdain the great heritage of China, but blesses it as the door through which he walked into the light.

The third reflection that strikes one on reading a work of conversion of an Oriental is that there is no difference whatever in the conversion of a Jew, a Greek, a slave or freeman, an Occidental or Oriental. The soil on which the grain of Eucharistic wheat falls may vary from country to country and from mind to mind, but the processes of development and growth and harvest are the same in all. The same melody is played on different instruments, but exactly the same laws of music and grace are obeyed. In every conversion there must be the intelligence which gives consent, the act or the will which commands adherence to the Truth that is revealed, and the grace which fecundates and generates supernatural life within the soul. These three processes were no different in St. Paul than they are in Paul Sih. God is the author of every conversion, and what is different in each instance is due solely to the background of the individual convert and to the immediacy of his reception of grace. All conversions and all deep piety, make the soul return to a kind of spiritual nihilism, in the sense that we realize that we have come from nothing and that if His sustaining hand failed to help us, we would fall back into that nothingness from which we came.

As the Psalmist says, "God is wonderful in His saints," and those who are interested in the greatest drama in all the world—namely the turning of a soul to Christ—will here find it acted out on an Oriental stage with an occasional scene from the Western world. May this story of a learned Chinese scholar and government official be the prelude to many other conversions in China, when Confucius, Mencius, Buddha, Küan-yin will take Chinese by their hands and lead them to the crib of Bethlehem.

+ *Fulton J. Sheen*
Auxiliary Bishop of New York

CONTENTS

xv

Contents

FROM CONFUCIUS TO CHRIST

"I am not one who was born in the possession of knowledge. I am one who loves the past and earnestly seeks to understand it" (Confucius, *The Analects*, VII, 19).

"I am the vine: you the branches. He that abideth in me, and I in him, the same beareth much fruit: for without me you can do nothing" (John 15:5).

I

Our Family

*"Whosoever shall do the will
of my Father that is in
heaven, he is my brother, and
sister, and mother"* (Matt.
12:50).

I was born in the vicinity of Shanghai in 1909. It
is hard for me to recall, much less to put into writing,
the history of my family. Suffice it to say here that
for generations my ancestors had lived on the outskirts of Nanking. At the time of the Tai-ping Rebellion, about one hundred years ago, my grandfather
brought our family to settle near Shanghai in the
place where I was born.

My Chinese name, "Kwang-tsien" (in English,
"Light Ahead") is derived from a Chinese maxim
which means, in its entirety, "To glorify ancestors and
enrich posterity." But another interpretation is that
a man should not concern himself only with living on
the surface, as it were horizontally, but should ponder
life vertically, keeping in mind that all forms of light
are a reflection of God, who is the "Light of the

World." But in spite of my religious name, I had a completely godless upbringing; no religious teaching of any sort, but in its place a folk religion in the shape of Buddhism and a very intensive training in pagan morality, highly exacting and idealistic.

I was delicate in health, and what is worse, at the age of five I contracted a kind of skin disease that made my head scabby. It was not cured until I was ten years old. I lived in a family with three elder sisters who looked upon me as a child to whom they were always kind, but about whom there was certainly nothing to admire. I was conscious of their pity because my scabby head deprived me of average good looks, and I had no special gifts of any kind to redeem my appearance. I was loved more by my grandmother than by anyone else, and I had a greater need of her warmth and devotion than the average child, who would have taken love for granted. Her demonstrative affection is still vivid in my memory. Even necessary severity came with difficulty to her. One day when she saw me doing something mischievous, she remonstrated with me: "You are not behaving yourself properly, my son."

I answered, "I know it."

"If you don't stop that," she warned, "I must be severe with you."

"I know it," I answered.

She spanked me. I said, "Grandma, you are spanking too high—on the bones!" (She wasn't hurting me a bit.)

She replied, "I know it."

My father, by contrast, was intensely reserved. He was a tall man and, though physically powerful, sedentary by habit. Not once in our lives did he ever play with me. His taciturnity was such that we children might have thought him a mute, except that once in a while he would utter one word: "Don't"—when my sisters and I were doing something he didn't like.

Having succeeded to my grandfather's business, he was a wine merchant. He had an excessive fondness for drink which was largely hereditary: it was said that when he was newly born he could scarcely breathe freely until he was fed a mouthful of wine, and he went to school with a bottle of wine hanging on his coat when he was only five years old.

Like the average Chinese, my father believed passionately in human progress and rejected all forms of supernatural religion as degrading superstition. He scarcely ever raised the question of religion as such, but sometimes he would remark that it was absurd for people to call themselves religious when they did not practise religion, and I often heard him say that it was wrong to influence children's minds in religious

5

matters, that they should be left to develop their own religious beliefs, or be permitted to have none at all if they chose. This does not mean that he himself was an atheist. Doubtless he had a personal belief of some kind that I was never able to learn. But I could observe that he was very kind and generous in his relations with other people. He never refused a request for charity. It seems to me that he was a faithful follower of Lord Chesterfield's precept: "Do not refuse your charity even to those who have no merit but their misery."

He was of an energetic temperament, and therefore very successful in business. It was one of his most marked characteristics that he never wasted time; he was convinced that success in any sphere of life comes to those who are not time-servers, but who make time serve them. For my part, it is difficult to estimate the debt I owe him. He gave me a good home; he set before me a constant example of plain living. For these reasons I felt impelled to love him, even though, when he was drunk, he often made me a servant of his outrageous whims.

I still remember that when I was thirteen years of age and was studying in a high school at Shanghai, my father once decided to punish me for receiving a report card from the school which bore the remark that, for reasons of health and safety, I should be warned not to do any more swimming in the pools near the school. My father considered this a report of grave misconduct and declared that I should be severely disciplined. I escaped bodily punishment only because I succeeded in hiding myself under a bed—at the expense of my stomach, for I had nothing to eat for almost twenty-four hours. In ordinary circumstances my father would never have got angry with me for such a thing; it was only because he was drunk and felt unhappy about the soaring price of wheat, the basic raw material of his wine business, that he made a scapegoat of me.

Of course, neither was I an innocent lamb. The moral law of China has ordained that the child must "honor the parent" unconditionally, and therefore a son has to accept subservient devotion on his part as an inevitable axiom of his life. So fully accepted is this that no Chinese has ever missed learning by heart a saying of Mencius, our great philosopher of the fourth century before Christ, who is the Chinese forerunner of those who throughout history have thought of the Cross as the key to life: "When heaven is about to confer a great responsibility upon a man it first exercises his mind with suffering, his bones and sinews with toil; it exposes his body to hunger, subjects him to extreme poverty, confounds his undertakings, and by all these methods stimulates his mind, hardens his

7

nature and makes good his incompetences." * Jere-
mias said in his Lamentations: "From above he hath
sent fire into my bones" (1:13). And in the book of
Wisdom we read: "Though in the sight of men they
suffered torments, their hope is full of immortality.
Afflicted in a few things, in many they shall be well
rewarded: because God hath tried them, and found
them worthy of himself. As in the furnace God hath
tested them, and as a victim of a holocaust he hath
received them" (3:4–6). Therefore I acknowledge
with all honesty that although my dislike of my
father's excessive drinking has had after-effects so
deep that to this day I can hardly bear to see anyone
overindulging in this way, it was from his hard discipline, no matter how unreasonable or disagreeable
or even unbearable it seemed at the time, that I
grasped the sense of humility and came to learn later
that the harder path really leads to a better life.

Indeed I have never felt that the rather rigorous
training I received at home put me under any handi-
cap, either in my childhood or in later life. At school,
although the youngest among my classmates, I was
always the leader, for I was full of ideas and driving
energy, and the self-control I had learned was recognized by my playmates, so that they accepted my

---

* Mencius, Book VI, ii, 15.

leadership without antagonism. And if I had not the benefit of a religious upbringing, at least I was given a deep sense of responsibility which made it a matter of urgency that I should develop a philosophy of life grounded on truth, independent of the traditions and habits of thought I found in my environment.

My native town is Tsing-pu, a little community famous for its fish products. As a small child my curiosity was aroused when I heard certain of the fishermen murmuring to themselves. I was told that they were Catholics and were praying in order to resist the devils. From this I derived the impression that Catholicism was a religion against evil and for the poor. Thus I had a definite opinion on the relation of the Catholic Church to the underprivileged long before I was clear as to what a Catholic might be.

At this point I must mention with deepest respect the late Lo Pa-hung, the Chinese St. Vincent de Paul, founder of hospitals and orphanages—builder on a foundation of poverty and sacrifice. I was too young to be his friend, but from my father and my school teacher I learned a great deal about his undertakings and his great influence in the community.

Lo was more commonly known among Westerners as the Chinese St. Joseph Cottolengo, for he established many a "little house" which—like the Piccola Casa in Turin—sheltered thousands of indigent sick.

9

He relied for financial help in his undertakings not upon the Church's purse, but upon free contributions received from day to day, especially from the poor. In case of need he always counted on the foster-father of Our Lord. St. Joseph is the holy patron of China, and Lo regarded him as his treasurer, who would never fail to supply him with all he needed for the cause of God.

Lo seemed to be the most learned man in the community and became the leader of the leaders. He often came to my town to carry out his apostolate, especially among the fishermen. Though, as I have explained, we were not religious people, my father nevertheless looked to him for guidance in spiritual matters, and his counsel was sought in all kinds of family problems—physical and financial. For this reason Lo's name was of frequent occurrence in our family talks.

Among the various stories concerning Lo, I was especially impressed by the one which showed his generous treatment of a prisoner. It goes this way: One day on his regular call at a prison in Shanghai he was told that a prisoner was about to be executed. He went into the cell and singled out the criminal from the group, a man with unkempt beard and tattered coat, and with a strange glitter in his eyes. Lo approached him and spoke to him with his usual

10

enthusiasm about the love of Christ, that he might prepare him for the next life by baptism.

"I am going to have my day tomorrow!" the prisoner cried. "What kind of devil are you to talk to me in this way today? Get out! Get out!" He howled like a maniac and slapped Lo's face with violence. Lo withdrew, but at the door, he turned back. He said: "Oh, I understand, it is tomorrow. It is quite all right. Never too late. God's door is always wide open. Call me when you want me."

The prisoner broke into a torrent of blasphemy— "I'll never want you, never, never, never!" The smile Lo turned on him was not merely the wise, understanding response of the great soul he was; it was in addition a good old-fashioned Chinese grin. His hand on the prisoner's elbow, he replied, with bubbling good nature: "Son, tomorrow you will, God's infinite mercy will see to that." Lo knew well that St. Francis de Sales never tired of saying that more flies are caught with honey than with vinegar.

The next morning he went to the place where the execution was to be held. Just a minute before the shooting was ordered, a great cry of "Have mercy on me, O God!" was heard. Without a doubt, the voice was that of the prisoner. Lo rushed to him at once, baptized him, and said: "My son, you are forgiven."

This story is only one of many. Of all the Chinese Catholic laymen distinguished for their charity, perhaps there is none of whom so many stories are told of extreme generosity to the poorest of the poor.

My family's reaction to Lo's generous heart and devoted charity was really profound. It was their consensus that Catholics were the best people they could make their friends; but unhappily they were persuaded of the incompatibility between Catholic doctrine and the traditional ancestral rites. As I look back now I acknowledge that it was this misunderstanding of the Catholic attitude toward our ancestral cults that kept my family completely outside the Church. And, in fact, this misapprehension has been the obstacle which separated the Catholic Church and Chinese society from the days of Father Matteo Ricci. At this point, I recall with a sense of gratitude the wise and courageous decision taken by His Holiness Pius XII who, at the outset of his pontificate, settled the question of the rites in such a way as to make it possible for Chinese converts to be loyal both to their traditional background and to their Christian faith.

II

Devotee of Küan Yin

"A voice of one crying in the desert: Prepare ye the way of the Lord, make straight his paths" (Mark 1:3).

If during my early years I had any religious concepts at all, they could possibly be traced to my grandmother. She was a zealous Buddhist and especially a worshipper of Küan Yin, the Goddess of Mercy. I remember that in the morning when I went to my grandmother's bedroom to ask for pocket money, I often saw her kneeling before the porcelain statuette of Küan Yin, praying fervently for her blessing. Since becoming a Catholic I have often been struck by the similarity of Küan Yin in posture to the mediaeval statues of the Blessed Virgin. On the nineteenth day of the Second Moon each year my grandmother kept a very rigid fast and ate nothing but a bowl of *congee*, in memory of Küan Yin's filial piety. Very often she said to me: "I have no hope in myself. My entire hope is in Küan Yin." And she would explain this as follows: "She watches continually over all who put their trust in her, and helps them. I am in no haste to die, but I am ready to depart when my time comes. I am comforted by the assurance that through the gracious help of Küan Yin I shall straightway enter into the future life."

If early religious influences have played a part in my conversion, it is this devotion of my grandmother's that left the deepest impression. Thus, in spite of my waywardness in my early childhood, I learned from her a profound respect for religion. I believed in prayer, though I seldom prayed; in supernatural help, though I seldom sought it. In later pages I shall testify as to how this instinctive impulse formed a mental ground on which I stood fast through many a crisis, and in the end was my preparation for seeing the Light.

What I admire about Küan Yin is her personality. Born a princess, she had the magnanimity to sacrifice all the comforts that life could furnish to a human being in order to search for the Love which would set herself and others free. Whether she actually found the Love is quite another question. To my mind, one of the reasons why Buddhism has been so popular in China is the cult of this feminine deity. I cannot dismiss it without mentioning the tremendous influence that its later development exercised upon my mind when I was a child, through the popular, touching

16

story of her self-forgetfulness. It runs as follows:

Once upon a time there was a Chinese king who had three beautiful daughters, the youngest of whom was Miao Shan. The king did not rule wisely or well, and his people suffered from his misgovernment, though this made no impression on his Majesty.

He determined upon the marriage of each of his princesses to a man of his choice. This was not an unusual way in the Orient of cementing political alliances. The two elder daughters fell in with the plan, but not Miao Shan. She refused, informing her father that she had taken a vow to dedicate her life to the service of humanity.

The king was enraged at his daughter's rebellion. She was condemned to go to a Buddhist nunnery, to a life of hardship and penury. This conformed perfectly to her fondest desires. She spent her days in labor among the people and her nights in the study of the Buddhist *sutras*, seeking enlightenment and the salvation of her soul. In her monastery, high amid the grandeur of the Incense Mountain, men forgot she was a princess, and remembered only that she was a servant of all in sorrow.

The king fell ill. The doctors could not cure him nor could the exorcists help him. The court sent for a great specialist, though whether in medicine or in witchcraft is not clear.

"Only a hand and an eye cut from a living human being will cure Your Majesty," declared the specialist solemnly.

Court circulars asking for an eye and a hand caused general consternation, but brought no result. Finally, a court messenger climbed the Incense Mountain and, calling upon this holy woman who knew no limits to her charity, told her of the king's need. Immediately she gouged out an eye and cut off a hand, and gave them to the messenger.

The king, strangely enough, was cured. Moved at last to feel gratitude for this extraordinary offering, he made a pilgrimage to the mountain top. He was astounded to discover his own daughter, to whom by a miracle the eye and hand had been returned. She refused his plea to come home, but exacted from him a pledge to devote himself henceforth to justice for his people.

Miao Shan, on the Incense Mountain, grew in holiness and spent herself in goodness towards all who appealed to her. Little wonder that when she died she was accepted by both heaven and earth as the Goddess of Mercy, the great Küan Yin.*

I do not know the original source of this story. What I can say is this, that Küan Yin is regarded by every Chinese, up to my generation, as the embodiment of the womanly virtues of beauty, mercy, and gentleness. Frequently images show her with a child in her arms. People do not reason concerning her: they love her. They may seek from her deliverance from

* John J. Considine, *Across a World* (Longmans), pp. 164–165.

danger, and she is much honored by mariners as their patron.

In my own case I realize now that the influence of Küan Yin on me has been much greater than I was aware of at the time. To begin with, I cherished the idea of salvation made possible through the intercession of the Bodhisattva (or "enlightened ones"), who had attained to the enlightenment of the Buddha but continued their existence in this world in order to rescue others. Associated with this was the concept of charity, which prepared me to understand later that there is a mysterious connection between suffering and love. Love and suffering, truly, are not separable. The experience of love is real and is not affected by suffering. All the same, sorrow remarries the soul to God. Therefore, we must suffer with joy and good humor. This is a discovery which sometimes makes me act so oddly that my friends think I have lost my mind; but actually, I have found my soul, and I would not now give it up for anything in all the world.

In the second place, the generous compassion of self-denial of Küan Yin impressed me profoundly. The salvation of others through the selflessness of the enlightened ones was made possible on the principle that merit could be transferred. Along with this went the idea that life is painful and that it is not limited to the individual life-span with which we are familiar, but the same suffering was lived out in other lives through the transmigration of souls. Obviously, the concept of transmigration is false; but the perception that between goodness and the divinization of souls there is some mysterious relation is fundamentally sound and salutary. It is a true sentiment attached to a false ideology.

Last, but not least, the popular Buddhist prayer: *Küan Yin, Goddess of Mercy, save the poor and the hapless, in the glory of Buddha,* was a solid mental foundation that enabled me to say very naturally the Angelical Salutation: *Hail Mary, full of grace! The Lord is with thee.*

What fascinated me in Küan Yin was her heroic renunciation of the world and her generous maternal love for all creation. Her cult prepared me for my interior predilection and passionate affection for the Mother. A Chinese proverb says: "When you drink the water, you must think gratefully of its source." Thus to a Chinese it is impossible to adore Christ without venerating the Blessed Virgin. How good God is to use my filial devotion to Küan Yin as an instrument for opening my eyes to see that *devotion to the Blessed Virgin is the touchstone of true Christianity!*

Generally speaking, the great majority of the Chinese have not been exclusively Confucian, Buddhist, or Taoist. They have been influenced by all of these systems—in ethical standards, in conceptions of the universe and of divine beings, and in beliefs about the future life. I was no exception. What had impressed me most in my early years was the practice of ancestor worship, which is still the popular cult, and well-nigh universal in China. In fact the real atheists in China are those who refuse to worship at the ancestral shrine. Nearly everything may be foregone and it will be forgiven, but this never.

In the spring especially at the Festival of Pure Brightness, people go out and worship at the graves on the hillsides; the tablets of the ancestors are preserved and honored in the clan temples and in the homes; the god of wealth is invoked at every Chinese New Year season, and, what is more, the kitchen god is besought to render a favorable report to Heaven on the family's conduct during the year. All these practices have depended upon a mixture of motives—respect and affection for the departed, fear, the desire for the prosperity of the living, and social usefulness. There have entered, too, the binding influence of custom and the desire thus to preserve the unity of the family and the clan.

Early in my life the experience of participating in this popular cult led me to the conclusion that it is inaccurate to term Chinese ancestor worship a religion, for in it the supernatural is hardly touched. Indeed, ancestor worship can be practised without conflict with belief in a Christian, Buddhist, or Mohammedan god, and I should even go so far as to say that the respect paid to fifteen-inch square wooden tablets inscribed with the names of ancestors is no more religious than that implied by the use of the picture of a great President on an American postage stamp. In its spirit, the celebration of the ancestor's birthday differs little from that of Valentine's Day or Mothers' Day in this country.

Perhaps the most characteristic feature of the Chinese folk religion, which Dr. Hu Shih has called Siniticism, is the practice known as *"Feng-shui"* (literally, in English, "wind and water"). It owes its origin to the dualistic system of *Yin* and *Yang*. Everything in nature is classified either as *Yin* or *Yang:* the earth, darkness, cold, femininity, maternity, weakness, death are all *Yin;* heaven, light, warmth, masculinity, paternity, strength, productivity, life are all *Yang.* The concept behind the system is that as man is the product of the forces of the universe, he must conduct himself in relation with the natural cosmic order. Accordingly, in the practice of *Feng-shui,* his institutions, his dwelling, and his burial place must be so arranged as to harmonize with the system. Temples, for example, face south (*Yang*), with protecting hills behind them and a water-course nearby (*Yin*). In its more rationalized form this idea of the close relation between human and natural phenomena leads to the conception that human conduct is reflected in acts of nature. Indeed the Chinese had recognized the relationship of forces in the natural environment to human behavior long before the Western peoples began their special studies in human biology and ecology.

For example, from early childhood every Chinese is greatly instructed by lightning, which is considered a chastisement sent by Heaven to punish those who disobey their parents, fail to finish the rice in their bowls, or throw waste paper on the ground. In the course of a solar eclipse, which symbolizes to the Chinese a struggle between the good (*Yang*) and the evil (*Yin*), it is incumbent upon all to assist by devout chanting the sun (*Yang*) in its ordeal with the moon (*Yin*). Under one aspect this can be interpreted as a combat between the good and evil principles in man. Thus *Yin Yang* and *Feng-shui* instilled in me the idea that man is so much a part of the natural order that improper conduct on his part will throw the whole of nature out of joint, and consequently my growing knowledge of the secrets of the universe through the study of natural sciences in my later years only increased my awe of the Creator.

The fact is that although China has never been a theocratic civilization, her cultural traditions have been, more than those of other nations, based on that principle of a perfect coordination between the heavenly and earthly orders which we call the Natural Law.

A further explanation is important. Among the original elements of the Chinese tradition are some which, no matter how shot through with superstition they have become, yet contain the residue of genuine social experience. For example, at a funeral the mourners dress in white, the corpse is dressed in clothes as new as possible, all the old clothes of the deceased are burned. Incense, candles and paper money are ignited and burned as a token of tribute and assistance to the dead. It is still my feeling that all these ideas and practices derive more from moral, educational and hygienic than from merely superstitious motives. The suffocating after-effects of burning "paper" money—which is made of tinfoil—may serve to kill germs. This seems a primitive makeshift in the modern view, but during thousands of years before the great scientist Pasteur was born it served its purpose well enough. The mode will be changed, but the principle remains.

In China there has been not a little of the observance of lucky and unlucky days. It is said that a child who is born on New Year's Day will inevitably become a beggar. Obviously this is not true. However, when I came to observe some of the great office buildings of New York City, equipped with the latest appliances for comfort and efficiency, in which there is a twelfth and a fourteenth floor but no floor numbered thirteen, I realized that in their anxiety to take advantage of the "lucky" and to avoid the "unlucky" the Chinese are not more backward than other peoples.

But this is irrelevant. The point is that from my early childhood I was brought up more or less as a Buddhist. I used to spend my spare time in a Buddhist temple near my home. I loved the Buddhist *sutras* and the whole monastic liturgy. The drums, the bells, and the wooden fish used by the monks in their religious services were my favorite joys, and the Five Hundred Lohans, or Arahats, Buddhist saints, who are known by their distinctive facial expressions, became my tried friends.

I do not pretend to have studied Buddhism, ancient and modern, except as presented to me by a few novels I read in my school days. Perhaps the reading of *Hsi Yu Chi* had some bearing on my admiration for the Buddhist priests. The book (translated into English by Arthur Waley under the title *Monkey*) is a fictional account of the adventures of Hsüan Chuang, a Buddhist saint, during his expedition to India in the

25

Tang Dynasty (A.D. 618–907) in search of sacred books and emblems. However, in my youth, Buddhism influenced me by two maxims known to everyone. The first is: "If I should refuse to descend into Hell [that is, in order to save souls], who will descend into Hell?" The second is this: "As soon as the butcher lays down his knife, he immediately becomes a Buddha." These generous ideals inspired me and prepared me to understand that the touchstone of the true religion is the belief in the Passion of Our Saviour and His boundless love for sinners. With Him we can commune, to Him we can pray and confess, from Him we can ask forgiveness of our sins, and in Him we can find our greatest peace.

Furthermore, one of the essential features of Buddhism is compassion for the Buddha. It is taught that there have been many Buddhas. One of the most generally represented is Gautama, or, more frequently in Chinese, Shih-chia-fo, or Shih-chia-mou-ni (Shakyamuni), the historic founder of the faith. As a rule he is represented as seated on a lotus in the attitude of meditation; sometimes as recumbent (the "Sleeping Buddha") as at the time of his death, when he is entering Nirvana; less frequently, as an ascetic, emaciated and unkempt. Probably even more popular is the Buddha Amitabha (O-mit'o-fo), through faith in whom, according to the widely prevalent teachings of the Pure Land (Ch'ing T'u) sect, entrance is to be had at death into the Pure Land, or Western Heaven.

Buddhism may be called a discipline of salvation which brings everything down to a very few simple truths—suffering and the cause of suffering, the truth concerning the extinction of suffering and the way to the extinction of suffering. All things are transitory, nothing permanent, and it is through attachment to the transitory—to sensual pleasures and the will to existence—that suffering arises. The way to salvation, therefore, is the way of detachment through asceticism; in perfect detachment is deliverance to an absolute good, not precisely defined.

The system, of course, contains no principle of divine grace which would make its asceticism more than a *via negativa*, nor is it to be thought that Buddha, the Enlightened One who has compassion on men and teaches them the way to deliverance, is worshipped as God. Nevertheless certain of its ideas influenced me in my youth to some extent and made me conscious from my early years that the world, both the seen and the unseen, is after all one universe, and that there is one Power or Being who ultimately controls it, and to whom appeal may be made. At the same time these concepts of Buddha's humanity caused me to be attracted in my mature years much more strongly to the mystical Incarnation in Catholi-

cism than to the vague character of God conceived
by modern liberal Protestantism.

Before concluding this chapter I must say something about Taoism, not that it influenced me as much
as Buddhism, but because it is so much an element of
the Chinese religious consciousness as inevitably to
have its bearing upon my spiritual background. The
first book I read was Laotse's Book of *Tao,* which
teaches the wisdom in the appearance of foolishness,
success under the appearance of failure, the strength
in weakness, the power of non-resistance, the futility
of contention for power. Let me quote one of his sayings which has impressed me most profoundly:

> "The Sage is good to the good,
> He is also good to the evil:
> For virtue is good in itself.
> The Sage is faithful to the faithful,
> He is also faithful to the unfaithful:
> For virtue is faithful in itself."*

And in another place he says: "High virtue is
unaware of its virtuousness, therefore it has virtue.
Low virtue is never free from virtuousness, therefore
it has no virtue."

In short, the central teaching of this book is that
moral excellence exists in proportion to obscurity;

---

* Chapter 49.

the best man is the one least observed, least distinguished, for only faults and mistakes draw attention
to the individual. It was a profound philosophy of
life, too difficult for me to understand. But what I
did grasp was this: the logic of Taoist teaching ran
counter to the logic of the world. Beyond this I understood no more, but it may well be that what I did
understand helped prepare my mind to perceive that
the wisdom of the world is folly with God.

III

Disciple of Confucius

"For amen I say unto you, till heaven and earth pass, one jot or one tittle shall not pass of the law, till all be fulfilled" (*Matt. 5:18*).

In my first year at elementary school I plunged into the well-known *San Tzu Ching,* or "Three-Character Classic," based on the fundamental concepts of Confucianism. The book is so called because each line consists of three characters only. The whole makes a pleasant jingle, easily remembered by the young boy. I then learned the whole poem off by heart, and when I could repeat it without error, I was instructed, line by line, in the meaning.

The subject matter of the poem is varied. In its total of just over 1,000 Chinese characters it provides elementary instruction in ethics. The first lines run:

> JEN CHIH CH'U
> HSING PEN SHAN
> HSING HSIANG CHIN
> HSI HSIANG YUAN

KOU PU CHIAO

HSIAN NAI CHIEN

CHIAO CHIH TAO

KUEI I CHUAN

and can be literally translated as follows:

"Men, one and all, in infancy are virtuous at heart;
  Their moral tendencies the same, their practice wide
     apart.
  Without instruction's friendly aid our instincts grow
     less pure;
  But application only can proficiency ensure."

The central theme of these opening lines taught me
the essential goodness of human nature. Some Christian scholars in the Western world raise against Confucius the objection that the somber concept of original sin is difficult to reconcile with this Confucian
view of the virtue of infancy. But the objection is
not valid, for Confucius also states that man has
ill-regulated desires which need to be disciplined. If
every human being in the world has certain libidoes
which need to be mastered, the obvious implication is
that something must have happened to human nature
at the origin of the race. Confucius does not presup-
pose these libidoes, but neither does he exclude them.
We are not as good as we ought to be: this is implicit
in Confucianism; so there is room in Confucianism for

an illumination from God to compensate for our weak nature. So early in my youth I learned from Confucian teaching that spirituality is not a place at which one arrives but a way one travels; the life-task of a "good-natured" man is the direction of energy to a higher ideal, a transcendent being. From this point of view, Confucius can be just as good a starting point for the discovery of Our Divine Master as Aristotle. Confucianism waits to be fulfilled as the Jewish law was fulfilled in Christ.

The second piece of literature I tackled was a work unique in Chinese literature. It, too, conforms to Confucian principles and is a poem with four characters to each line and running, for the most part, in couplets. It consists of exactly 1,000 characters, and the singularity of the composition is that no character is repeated. It is related that an imprisoned scholar-statesman was promised Imperial pardon if he could so arrange the cards bearing 1,000 different characters used in the teaching of the Imperial heir as to make continuous sense. He succeeded, but the effort, in a single night, turned his hair white. The *Ch'ien Tzu Wen* ("Thousand Character Composition") is his arrangement. Two couplets may be quoted as samples of this work:

> "To virtuous rulers once 't was given
> To see good omens sent by Heaven."

> "In composition, terseness seek;
> With clearness ever strive to speak."

The opening lines impressed me with the thought that human nature inclines us to conceive the notion of divinity. For me they anticipated in some way St. Thomas' dictum: "Nature inclines us to love God, its Author, more than ourselves; otherwise the natural inclination would be perverse, and it would not be perfected, but destroyed, by charity." *

It was in my eleventh year that I began to study the whole course of "the Confucian Canon." It is composed of the "Four Books" (*Ssu Shu*) and the "Five Classics" (*Wu Ching*).† It can readily be understood that for a little boy the comprehension of the complete work is no easy task. But as no Chinese education is considered complete without a thorough grasp of it, everyone has to study it very hard.

In these great works, Confucius discussed in the main human nature and human problems, man's rela-

---

* *Summa Theologica* IIa, IIae, q.26, a. 3.

† The "Four Books" are: (1) "The Great Learning" (*Ta Hsüeh*); (2) "The Doctrine of the Mean or Middle Way" (*Chung Yung*); (3) "The Analects or Sayings of Confucius" (*Lun Yü*); (4) "The Works of Mencius" (*Mêng Tzû*). The "Five Classics" are (1) "The Book of Changes" (*I Ching*); (2) "The Book of History" (*Shu Ching*); (3) "The Book of Poetry" (*Shih Ching*); (4) "The Book of Rites" (*Li Chi*); (5) "Spring and Autumn Annals" (*Ch'un Ch'iu*).

tion to the family, the state and the world—education, government, and law. As a result, ancient China produced a great civilization with highly developed theories of human nature, moral conduct and political organization, but, in the meantime, it was primitive in its religious and theological thinking and spent little time in speculation about life after death. In this sense, preoccupation with man and his life in this world is the essential feature of Confucianism. Confucius taught a philosophic doctrine which has been interpreted as similar to Plato's theory of ideas. A sincere Confucianist would be recognized as a good man in any civilization.

My five years' study of the Confucian Canon taught me that the core of Confucius' teaching is self-discipline and self-perfection, which can be attained by the virture of "setting the conscience right." So the essential principle of all the great works of Confucius consists in enlightening one's moral sense, in converting others, and in attaining the goal of perfection. In other words, the moral improvement of one's own person through the purification of one's own conscience is the root or starting-point of all achievement. But although his doctrines relate chiefly to the relationship between man and man, they are far from devoid of an element higher than mere humanism. The powers of the unseen world have their

acknowledged part in controlling the spirit of man
in his duty to his fellows. As Christopher Dawson
points out, "the difference between the religious and
the irreligious is not a difference between levels of
culture but a difference between levels of consciousness." *

Actually Confucius betrays an awareness of God
when he says: "One who gives offence to Heaven has
nowhere to expiate his sins." Does he not anticipate
the words of the Gospel: "Believe me, there is pardon
for all the other sins of mankind and the blasphemies
they utter; but if a man blasphemes against the Holy
Spirit, there is no pardon for him in all eternity; he
is guilty of a sin which is eternal" (Mark 3:28–30)?
To my mind, all the wisdom of Confucius comes from
his faith and confidence in Heaven, which, it seems
to me, is only another name for God.

But it is especially his emphasis on filial piety
which has deeply impressed me. The fact is that filial
piety, which is regarded as "the first of all the
virtues," is the core of Confucius' teaching. The
Chinese word for "culture" or "religion," *chiao*, is
derived from the word for "filial piety," *hsiao*, written with the sign for "filial piety" plus a causative
radical (meaning "making filial"). Now unhappily
the virtue of filial piety, misapprehended, can degen-

* *Religion and Culture* (Sheed and Ward), p. 41.

38

erate in practice into a form of magnified family selfishness at the cost of the public interest. How far is this from the teaching of Confucius! "The reason why the gentleman teaches filial piety," he says, "is not because it is to be seen in the home and everyday life. He teaches filial piety in order that man may respect all those who are fathers in the world. He teaches brotherliness in the younger brother, in order that man may respect all those who are elder brothers in the world. He teaches the duty of the subject, in order that man may respect all who are rulers in the world." Again he says: "Those who love their parents dare not show hatred to others. Those who respect their parents dare not show rudeness to others." In the book *Li Chi* he is reported as saying to a duke: "The man of true humanity serves Heaven as his parents, and serves his parents as Heaven." Although I did not have any supernatural common sense, it was not hard for me to realize even then that the nascent theism of Confucius should not be allowed to degenerate into pantheism. As St. John says, if one's love is genuine, a love in deed and in truth, such love, whether one is aware of it or not, is an affirmation of God.

Is it not clear that for Confucius filial piety is the centre and pivot of all goodness? Is it not also clear that it is because filial piety is deeply rooted in the hearts of the Chinese people, that China has been fertile soil for the seed of the Catholic Church? To my mind a good Confucianist is by nature a Catholic, for in all the world there is no single society where filial piety and brotherly love take a more eminent and more universal place than in the Catholic Church, and where Paternal Authority is more nobly represented and more abundantly generous than in the Supreme Pastor in his office of Vicar of Jesus Christ.

I must point out, here, that Confucius was no prophet, he claimed no new revelation. He was a traditionalist par excellence, one who prided himself on being "a transmitter and not an originator." He knows himself to be incompetent to discuss spiritual problems, and his inherent honesty is based on truth; but he is not discouraged, he wants to leave open the possibility of another knowledge with which he was not acquainted, namely the supernatural knowledge which comes from Faith. For example, he says in the "Book of Songs":

> "The presence of the Spirit;
> It cannot be surmised.
> How may it be ignored?"

Again, asked by a follower how to serve the spirits of the departed, he put the question aside with the rejoinder: "You are not yet able to serve man; how, then, can you serve the spirits?" When asked to discuss death, he retorted: "While you do not know life, what advantage is there in discussing death?"

Concerning these statements some Western Christian thinkers maintain that Confucius is not referring to God. To me it is crystal clear that Confucius more often mentions God than many of the Western textbooks on ethics. It is true that Confucius admitted that since we can know very little about ourselves, we can know little about the Spirit. However, this does not necessarily mean a denial of the Spirit but only of the adequacy of human reason. Confucius was the contemporary of the prophets of Israel. Lacking the Providential guidance afforded the Jews before the coming of the Savior, he could not pierce the future and speak of the supernatural life with certitude.

Another great thinker of China who exercised a deep influence upon me is Motse. He lived from 468 B.C. to 401 and was roughly one century behind Confucius. Among all Chinese philosophers, he comes closest to the Christian teachings, for he alone teaches universal love as the basis of society and of peace, shows that Heaven loves the people equally, and insists on the belief in the existence of the spirits. What I thought of God then may be gathered from a most beautiful passage of Motse which, though I read it about thirty years before my conversion to the Catholic faith, is still very deeply impressed upon my mind:

To obey the will of Heaven is to accept righteousness as the standard. To oppose the will of Heaven is to accept force as the standard. . . . The will of Heaven to me is like the compass to the wheelwright and the square to the carpenter. . . . I know Heaven loves man dearly not without reason. Heaven ordered the sun, the moon, and the stars to enlighten and guide them. Heaven ordained the four seasons, Spring, Autumn, Winter and Summer, to regulate them. Heaven sent down snow, frost, rain, and dew to grow the five grains and flax and silk so that the people could use and enjoy them. Heaven established the hills and rivers, ravines and valleys, and arranged many things to minister to man's good or bring him evil. Heaven appointed the dukes and lords to reward the virtuous and punish the wicked, to gather metal and wood, birds and beasts, to engage in cultivating the five grains and flax and silk to provide for the people's food and clothing. Suppose there is a man who is deeply fond of his son and has used his energy to the limit to work for his benefit. But when the son grows up he returns no love to the father. The gentlemen of the world will all call him unmagnanimous and miserable. Now Heaven loves the whole world universally. Everything is prepared for the good of man. The work of Heaven extends to even the smallest things that are enjoyed by man. Such benefits may indeed be said to be substantial, yet there is no service in return. And they do not even know this to be unmagnanimous. This is why I say the gentlemen of the world understand only trifles but not things of importance.*

But it is to that great disciple of Confucius, Mencius, with his inspired longing for the "Good Shepherd of Peace," that my mind returns when I seek the most striking symbolic foreshadowing, in the Confucian tradition, of the Redeemer. "In the whole of the Empire," he declares boldly, "there is no shepherd of men who does not love to send men to their deaths." And "If there should be found a head of a state who does not love to send men to their deaths, the peoples of the world would lift up their heads, aspiring to enjoy his rule. They would run to him as water which of its own accord flows toward the valleys. Who could withstand such a torrent?"

In a word, although in my early years I learned from Confucianism only a system of ethics based upon man's nature as a social being, not upon religion, I had even then an indistinct vision of the door through which I should walk into the light. Therefore, for me, the Confucian teaching is a natural foundation-stone

---

* Lin Yutang, *The Wisdom of China and India* (Random House), pp. 233, 235.

to the supernatural edifice of the Church. I have often said to myself and to my Catholic compatriots, "In the history of China there is no man as great as Confucius because there is no man as filial towards God."

It is all so clear to me now. Although there is no lack in the works of Confucius of sayings which revealed to me his limitations, his religious belief is a simple belief. It postulated nothing. It put no obstacles in His way. It is incorrect, therefore, to speak of Confucius as an irreligious man: irreligious he is only as one who refuses to believe in any specific revelation. Confucius always believed in God, but preferred not to say so, for fear of being misunderstood. Confucius believed in God, the most common designation of Him in his teachings being the term "Heaven," or the "Creator of Things." But Confucius was honest enough to leave the Creator of Things in an aura of mystery, entertaining for Him a kind of awed piety and reverence.

In fact, Confucianism at the time of Christ's birth was a thing of grandeur, evidencing by the character it produced in the best of the Chinese how fit an instrument it was for the work which the coming of Christ should complete. It seems to me, therefore, that the Confucian system is not merely a testimony to the intellect's power of drawing inferences of the divine from the external universe; everything in Confucianism was preparatory, looked forward to something which should complete it. His teaching was not a consummation; it was a preparation, a hard and heavy preparation: not maturity, but a superb training for maturity. Maturity came upon Christ's birth, that all things might be re-established in Him. It is in this sense that St. Augustine says that the history of the race is the story of one man. We Chinese must take Confucius as our point of departure in order to arrive at Christ, for only the Gospel of Christ can fulfill the doctrine of Confucius.

IV

Bible Class

*"This people honoureth me
with their lips: but their heart
is far from me. And in vain
do they worship me, teaching
doctrines and commandments
of men"* (Matt. 15:8–9).

My first approach to Christianity was made in the
Shanghai High School. It was a private school, and
there were many Protestant missionaries on the fac-
ulty, among them one elderly Englishwoman who
taught geography. I do not know to which of the
Protestant sects she belonged. In any event, she showed
greater energy in preaching the Gospel than in teaching geography. Students were warmly welcomed to
Bible classes at her home, and their attendance at
these classes in large measure determined their marks
in geography. Yet this was not the only attractive
consideration. Her simple life, sympathetic attitude,
and unfailing charity towards the poor warmed our
young hearts. As a worshiper of Küan Yin, as well as
a Confucianist who had a favorable background for

the reception of the teachings of Christ, I voluntarily attended the Bible classes almost regularly.

I seemed to her a promising student who showed a willingness to accept Christianity. For my own part, my interest in Christian doctrine grew to such extent that I unconsciously became dissatisfied with what she taught. Naturally, I had no penetrating theological questions on tap to disconcert her with. I could not even think of any particular problems I wanted solved. What bothered my mind was the question of the existence of God. I wavered uneasily between the notion that there must be some sort of a God and the feeling that I was addressing thin air.

There were times when I honestly tried to pray. I asked the teacher about this, and she told me about having a "religious experience." I sat quietly in my room over a period of many weeks, an hour or so at each attempt, and waited for something to happen. When nothing happened, I felt that the teacher must be a fraud to be going around telling students such rubbish about God "talking" to one. She seemed to be such a sincere person, however, that I could not quite believe this of her. She always listened very quietly and attentively to everything I said and was composed and gentle in her answers. Finally I gave this up, overcome by impatience and concluding that she was sincerely deluding herself.

One day, however, I raised the question of the existence of God and called for a thorough discussion of it. I had no quarrel with the ideology of Christendom; what dissatisfied me in Protestantism was the same thing that dissatisfied me in Confucianism. I did not want a notion of Him merely in imaginary and metaphorical terms. I demanded the demonstration of His existence in an absolute way.

At that time I was much troubled in spirit, feeling that the ocean on which I had embarked was a trackless waste. I sought for certainty. I had been oppressed and disheartened when I found, in the Bible classes, that the quest for it was futile. I was trying to reach land, the solid land of truth, the paradise of love and faith that should declare itself by tokens plainer and more commanding than the pale and glimmering reflection in my own vacillating mind and conscience. I had discovered, in common with the voyagers in Browning's "Paracelsus," that the real heaven was always beyond.

During the course of the discussion I had precipitated, I stated that if one could only conceive of Him as a metaphorical abstraction, a synonym for nature stripped of all personality, there was practically no difference between Protestantism and Confucianism, and surely there was no one in Heaven to Whom one could pray. If one could not apprehend His Presence,

51

He could only be an abstraction, a black blur in the sky, a great "universal unconsciousness," difficult to grasp as a genuine reality. Truth was like life, I added, it had to be taken in its entirety or not at all. In fact, I was confronted with the same mystery, primary and profound, that I had entertained since my early years. *Ex nihilo nihil*, as the Latin tag of school days has it: Nothing can come from nothing.

The teacher took my argument to be an attack of the most irresponsible and offensive nature; consequently it invited a hell-fire challenge from her. "Does it mean nothing to you," she said in trembling tones, "that if you reject Christ, you will be burnt in hell?"

My good intention had been wholly mistaken. However, I accepted the challenge. I smiled as I replied: "If, as you say, my ancestors are all in hell at this moment, it would be unfilial of me not to be willing to suffer with them. Besides, if heaven is full only of white men, I should be very uncomfortable there. I had better go to hell, where the Chinese are."

School in China has always meant much more discipline and much less fun than it has in America, and my sarcastic answer cancelled all previous credits. Poor soul, she never anticipated such a rude repercussion from one of her favorites. Even at this moment I cannot think without a sense of shame that on hearing my atheistic retort she came close to fainting.

Here I shall leave this incident, so painful to the respected teacher and to the school—and to myself, since I was in fact an admirer of both. However, I must confess now that it was because I could not grasp the idea of the supernatural last end that I failed to obtain the special inspiration to which the gifts of the Holy Ghost would render me docile.

As a result of this unhappy incident I was honorably dismissed from the school. At the time my father had died, and therefore I was free of any discipline. The following year I transferred to the Nanyang Middle School at Shanghai.

From that year, I recall most vividly the reading of the *Ma Shih Wen Tung*, which is a systematic study of Chinese grammar, and to my knowledge the only modern grammar of the Chinese language in existence. Its author, Ma Hsiang Po, a very distinguished Catholic, was the founder of two Chinese universities. The source of my delight in this book was the discovery of certain fundamental principles in the Chinese language. My passion for it became such that I saw the author in my dreams. Not until 1933, when he proposed the formation of a National Salvation Association at Shanghai after the Manchuria Incident, did I have the opportunity of making his acquaintance, and I have always regretted the fact that my youth—I was then twenty-four—made it difficult for me to become a friend of this remarkable man, who was ninety-four at that time.

Now, to return to my story: In 1926 Shanghai was full of student revolutionaries, planning utopias to be reached through blood and fire. At first I held aloof. But having become convinced that the Chinese war-lord system was rotten to the core and should not survive, I pondered how it should be overthrown. In my view, the only Chinese who really understood China's needs was Chiang Kai-shek, leader of the Kuomingtang Revolutionary Army. The thing to do, therefore, was to join the Kuomingtang Party. At eighteen, in Shanghai, I did so.

I did good underground work in the school and in its vicinity. I had no time for religion in those days. My great preoccupation was how to become a good party worker. It was in 1927, the year of my graduation from the Nanyang Middle School, that the Kuomingtang Party came to power. I was appointed Party Secretary to the district of Soochow in the neighborhood of Shanghai. I remained very active on party business, and largely owing to my efforts many labor unions were organized. Although at the time the Kuomingtang Party had already begun to adopt an independent political course from the Communist line, the social order was very much influenced by Marxian materialism. There were ever and anon strikes and agitations. As a party worker I should have cooperated with the local government authorities to relieve the situation, but I paid no attention to it, pretending that it contained no dangers.

One man who influenced my life at that time was Mr. Y. T. Wang, Mayor of the municipality of Soochow, who had taught me Chinese literature in the Nanyang Middle School at Shanghai. He had a deep interest in political philosophy and communicated his interest to me. We became devoted friends. He was not a Christian, but I am quite sure that Christ had said to him: "Love your enemies; do good to them that hate you: and pray for them that persecute and calumniate you." One day he asked me to dinner with him. In a very gentle tone he said: "What do you think about the present trouble in this city? To me it seems that the trouble is more fundamental than a mere moment of disturbance. It is full of hate and bitterness and hunger and waste and sorrow. But why? The political direction of the Kuomingtang Party is not based on the principle that more hate and less love makes for a better world. We, the Chinese people, cling to our belief in what we call civilization, which really only means that we do not favor pushing people around, that we do not exact hate, and that we do want to love and be loved."

As a teacher and a veteran party member as well,

he could hardly be challenged by me. From the look on his face I understood that he wanted to give me an extracurricular lesson. Thus he continued: "Water is stronger than fire, and yet fires continue to destroy; water can win its victory only when the fire is sought for, discovered, and scientifically combated. Happy people are never materialists. Revolution springs only from discontent, misery and hate. If through our own stupidity we drive the masses to desperation we have only ourselves to blame. As my student and my dearest friend I wish that you should devote your life to the constructive work of our revolution and to the task of cultivating love and diminishing hate."

That conversation must have taken place more than twenty years ago, but the words impressed me so profoundly that they have been ringing in my ears ever since. That night I felt harassed and could not go to sleep. I came to an overwhelming sense of how much time and how many energies I had wasted on these things which could only contribute to the force of destruction. Next morning I decided to resign from my party office and, in accordance with the advice and with the financial help of Mr. Wang, I entered Soochow University to receive my college education.

This made it possible for me to have my second encounter with Christianity. Soochow University was a sound Methodist institution near Shanghai, the type of school that believed in fundamental education and instilled precepts of severe self-discipline. As I recall my freshman year, it was a period of quiescence. To my studies I brought a good, if not a brilliant mind. I won high honor, and my scholastic index was just a little under 3.00 (which meant that I had got an A in practically every course).

I was not much given to athletics, although I played tennis expertly. I liked basketball, but my eyesight was poor—I had worn glasses from boyhood—and I never became proficient in the sport. I became immersed in secular studies and gave little time to thinking about religion. Life was busy; I had no serious troubles, and success in my courses came with surprising ease. As far as anything spiritual went, I was just waltzing along—not searching, not interested, not even aware that anything was missing.

I confess that my mind was so occupied with the whirl of studies and events that my memory preserved but a vague impression of my earlier religious inclinations. In fairness to my alma mater, I must say that religious education was by no means ignored in the curriculum. There was in the University a professor who was a frequent subject of discussion among my schoolmates. He taught religion and was, of all things, a Methodist pastor. We talked about him earnestly, for we could find no fault in him. He was quiet and aloof, and we never could decide just how a man so intelligent and so admirable could have found anything in Protestantism to attract him and keep him from joining the herd of non-believers. Once a week we had two hours of religious instruction, and among some forty classmates there was one who usually called himself an atheist. Instead of attending religion class, the "atheist" would always go to a nearby tea-house of doubtful reputation, where he attained some proficiency at billiards and got his primary education in the subject of commercial love. He was a generous boy and would report on his experiences to the other members of the class at the end of each religious period. I must say that we really did enjoy his reports more than the religious instruction we had in the classroom. On my own part I felt that I had given religion a chance, and that Christ had been a failure from the beginning. I felt I had intellectual proof that there was no God; there was nothing left but to make of life the most one could.

To the best of my recollection, it must have been somewhere during the course of my second year in college that the God-ache came upon me and the desire for religion began to make itself felt in the recesses of my mind.

The painful incident in my high school Bible class had left me with a sense of remorse, and this combined with the conciliatory spirit learned from my benevolent teacher, Mr. Wang, to urge me into making a comfortable truce with Protestantism. Although I was still unable to find an explanation of life—its purpose and direction, the ultimate spiritual realities, the relation of the person with God—to fill the spiritual vacuum left by Confucius, I began, strangely enough, to love the practice of attending Sunday morning services and did so with considerable frequency. I liked the singing of hymns before the services began, notwithstanding that the services were more social than spiritual.

Why this impulse to worship suddenly came to me remains a matter of speculation. Neither faith nor theology could have produced it; there was no belief in my mind, no system of theology offered by the Protestantism with which I was acquainted. One possible explanation is the sort of religious inferiority complex I had, which led me to submit to my superiors, setting aside my desire for full knowledge. Another is that almost all the Protestant teachers in the University led devout lives, thus setting a living example for me to follow. But there is the further possibility that I clung to Protestantism as a kind of compromise with the way of life which I was powerless to halt; in my heart I did not believe in its tenets at all.

59

At best, my attitude towards Protestantism had hitherto been what diplomats call "a benevolent neutrality." In speaking to my friends I often compared this attitude to that taken towards the early Church by Gamaliel—that most amiable of the Pharisees. Notwithstanding the fact that I prayed often, my prayers were more or less based on the belief that actually everything was determined by various conditions—heredity, environment, chance, biological and economic factors. I was completely ignorant of God's love, and I thought of Him only as a merciless, stern judge. The god to whom I prayed in my state of vagueness was assuredly very different from the one worshipped by my Protestant teachers and classmates. I realized later that though Protestants claim the same Gospel, they give it different interpretations, and inevitably they cherish their different concepts of God.

All these reflections may be summed up in these terms: I was unable to put my finger on any part of Christianity and declare with certainty that here I found a difficulty; but I was entirely certain that something was wrong. Since becoming a Catholic I have grasped the fact that, apart from the Incarnation, man could know God only as Infinite Power, and could have, with regard to the meaning of His infinity, only a shadowy notion—or no notion at all. It is only when man "sees what the Church sees" * that he can love what she loves.

Because of my lukewarm attitude towards religion my sophomore year ended with no further scholastic honors. To my great sorrow I got a barely passing mark for religion—at least I was sorry about it in those days, but subsequent reflection and the fuller knowledge I now possess have convinced me that I was fortunate in my disappointment. I voluntarily transferred to the Comparative Law School of China in Shanghai, which, although a part of Soochow University, was under the Presidency of Dr. John C. H. Wu, of whom I shall speak later. The law school had a much less Protestant atmosphere. I felt rather comfortable to leave my "religion" behind me in this way.

---

* F. J. Sheed, *Theology and Sanity*, p. 1.

V

My Professor

"He that doth truth cometh to the light, that his works may be made manifest: because they are done in God" (John 3:21).

It was not until 1934 that I had my first encounter with Catholicism, and then I observed its externals first. In that year I went to Italy to do graduate work at the University of Rome, and I remained there for several years. In my leisure hours I had much opportunity to acquaint myself with the great works of art in the Eternal City, and with the beauty of Catholic life in its liturgical expression, and I derived from my experience an admiration for the accomplishment of the Church; but, more especially, it struck me that here one had hold of something concrete, in contrast to abstractness of Protestantism.

My first intimation of the interior aspects of Catholicism coincided with a visit I made to Florence, during the course of my University studies, for in this picturesque, beautiful and romantic city I made the acquaintance of Dante. Now no one in his senses would go to Dante to learn the truths of Catholic doctrine for the first time; unless he knows what the book contains, so to speak, before he opens it, he will never find out. As a matter of fact, for me, Dante's influence made itself felt, not with specific reference to the Catholic faith, but by introducing me into the element, as it were, of supernatural religion. For the first time I saw the holiness of beauty, and the beauty of holiness. His real interpretation of mystical humanism suggested an answer to the problem of the Other World which Confucius had scrupulously avoided and provided me with a foundation of Christian theology which became a source of instruction and inspiration.

Furthermore, in his appreciation of antiquity, Dante took the traditional mediaeval view, which respected and praised ancient civilization as an instrument of divine providence and as a secular prelude to the drama of man's redemption. This idea served as an incentive to me to re-appraise the actual and perennial value, the significance and authority of the pre-Christian achievements of all the great Chinese philosophers, thus reintegrating me with the Chinese tradition.

When I was studying in the University of Rome, I was under the direction of Professor Alberto de'Stefani. One of the foremost economists in Italy, he had served as the first Minister of Finance under Mussolini's regime from 1922 to 1923. It was owing to his efforts that the Italian economy, shattered after World War I, was saved from deterioration and the deficit in the national budget finally reduced.

When Mussolini challenged the authority of de'Stefani's administration in maintaining the integrity of the national budget, de'Stefani chose resignation instead of compromise. He was made to understand that his popularity with Mussolini was at a low ebb, and was "kicked upstairs" to become Minister of State and a member of the Grand Council of Fascism, which was supposed to be the Politburo of the Fascist regime. He held the post long enough to take part in the significant decision of July 24, 1943, in which the Grand Council of Fascism called for Mussolini's resignation. For this he was sentenced to death by Mussolini in Verona and narrowly escaped Ciano's fate. But in recognition of his valuable contributions to his country in the economic and financial fields and his last desperate effort to overthrow Mussolini, he was ultimately cleared of all civil and war responsibilities by the Italian judicial courts.

While I was a student in his department of the University he was my dear and honored teacher. It is impossible to record all I learned from him. He did me unnumbered kindnesses. It was he who, besides untiring efforts to guide me in the study of economics, spared no energy at any time and in any place he deemed fit to lead me to embrace the Faith. My education would have been but a thin and poor thing had I missed the great experience of this association. The things Professor de'Stefani did for me in the sphere of religion even gratitude cannot enumerate or remember. It appeared to me that he could not find anyone near him without interesting himself in that person's spiritual welfare.

It was he who prepared me to understand that what modern Western thinkers such as August Comte, Ludwig Feuerbach, Friedrich Nietzsche and Karl Marx offer us is not the divine beauty—which they scoff at—but the Tower of Babel, a civilization built without God, not aspiring to heaven but striving to reduce heaven to the level of earth. When I came across Comte's Positivism in my reading and pondered his dictum, so typical of the nineteenth century, that "from the very nature of the human mind every branch of our knowledge has necessarily to pass through three successive theoretical states: the theological or fictitious state, the metaphysical or abstract state, and the scientific or positive state," there was no shadow of doubt in my mind that this century must reverse the process if our civilization is to survive. So

68

even then I had the knowledge which helped me later to see clearly that Marxist Communism, which has plunged humanity into the limestone lake of materialism in which rationalism and positivism alike are drowned, aims only at making man less than a man by reducing him to a tool, while Christianity is destined to make man more than a man by making him a child of God.

Under Professor de'Stefani's guidance I wrote a thesis entitled "The Economic and Financial Reforms of Italy after World War I," in which I gave in detail all that de'Stefani had accomplished during his tenure of office as Minister of Finance. The thesis happened to be read by the late General Tsiang Pai-li, who was so much interested that he recommended to the government that Professor de'Stefani be invited to China to serve as high adviser in charge of economic and financial reforms. This invitation was issued and accepted, and General Tsiang and I were designated as de'Stefani's collaborators.

The work began in February 1937, but it was brought to an end by the Japanese invasion of China in July of the same year. Although the invasion prevented the accomplishment of our program of reform, these months were not without profit, especially for me. Perhaps the outstanding merit of the advice submitted by de'Stefani from the agricultural point of view was the persuasive evidence he offered in refutation of the prophets of doom who envisioned world-wide starvation through overpopulation. He pointed out that the root cause of China's continuing poverty and low standard of living was her failure to use adequately the natural advantages and resources with which she is so richly endowed. In densely populated Italy, he noted, population increase was accompanied by an increasing rather than a decreasing per capita income. Advance in technology and science overcame the depressing effect of population increase. It was his opinion that if in China full and intelligent utilization were made of soil, water, climate, wasteland, minerals and forests—and, above all, manpower—the standard of living could be raised to compare favorably with that of any modern nation. To his mind, therefore, the social and economic policy of China should be planned with reference to an increasing rather than a decreasing population. The foundation should be agrarian reform, beginning with a radical program of rent-cutting; then industrial development. On these grounds he flatly rejected the Liberal argument for birth control as a preventive of "population explosion," terming it an immoral act against nature and a means in fact to race suicide.

The result of this experience for me was that thus early in my career, it became clearly established in my mind that it would be preposterous to suppose that, in a universe governed by law, the practice of birth control could be anything except harmful to society and to the individual. At the time, however, I did not know this was the position taken by the Catholic Church.

VI

Failure of a Mission

> *"It is not of him that willeth,
> nor of him that runneth, but
> of God that sheweth mercy"*
> *(Rom. 9:16).*

Although I was wholly unaware of it, another influence was bringing me a further step towards Rome at this time. As I have said, participating in Professor de'Stefani's work also was General Tsiang Pai-li. He was an able assistant; but, more than this, by his character he was the greatest of teachers.

General Tsiang needs no identification for any Chinese. President of the National Military Academy, the Chinese West Point, he was one of the foremost strategists of China. His sudden death, a few days after his fifty-seventh birthday, in 1939, came as a shock to a host of friends and admirers in the spheres of literature, government and education, in all three of which he had played an active and important part.

He was born into a staid, middle-class family in Hai-ning, a staid, middle-class town in Chekiang. He has been described as possessing, at a very early age,

75

a markedly sympathetic disposition and a great spirit of self-sacrifice, displaying a filial piety rarely observed in young boys. For example, before I knew him personally, I had been deeply impressed by hearing of the following incident, which occurred when he was fourteen.

One day his mother was so seriously ill that no medical remedy seemed effective, and it was thought that her days were numbered. Almost everyone in the family was ready to despair, except Pai-li. He was well acquainted with the story of Küan Yin and remembered the extraordinary filial piety which had been expressed by the sacrifice of a portion of her own flesh to heal her father. The thought came to him that the method should not fail in his mother's case.

He went to the kitchen and, without any hesitation and unnoticed by anyone, cut a piece of flesh from his left arm and put it into the pot in which the Chinese medicine, in the form of a soup, supposed to be the last resort for his mother, was being prepared. Strangely enough, after the medicine had been administered his mother was cured. His conduct came to light only when his bandaged arm could no longer escape the attention of others during the hot summer days.

Such an act, it may be, seems humdrum in modern eyes; in the light of eternity, it is exciting enough.

General Tsiang went first to Japan and then to Germany for his military training. After he returned to China in 1908 he served as Chief of Staff of the Chinese Army in Manchuria. It was he who laid down the first blueprint for national defense in the northeastern part of China. After that his rise was rapid. In 1912, at the age of thirty, he became President of the Pao Ting Military Academy, of which most of today's outstanding military leaders, Communists as well as Nationalists, are graduates.

In his political career he was a close associate of Yuan Shih-kai, the first President of the Republic of China, who seems to have been greatly attracted to the General with his background of military distinction.

As internal dissension grew and war clouds gathered over the young Republic, General Tsiang had to keep his naturally strong passion for public duty under stern control and lead a rather secluded life, engaging himself entirely in literary research work. When the Kuomingtang Party came to power in 1927 he remained on the outside looking in. This was understandable. He was not a member of the Kuomingtang Party and he was especially opposed to the Kuomingtang Party policy of unifying China through military force. Was General Tsiang to be asked to do what he did not believe in? His turn had to wait until the threat of Japanese invasion induced Generalissimo Chiang Kai-shek to call into his administration other patriots who were not members of the Kuomingtang Party, such as Dr. Hu Shih, to do what they did believe in. General Tsiang did his part. In fact, during the Sian Incident in 1936 he shared the fate of Generalissimo Chiang Kai-shek when the latter was kidnapped by the Communist sympathizer, General Chang Hsueh-liang. In his published diary Generalissimo Chiang acknowledges that General Tsiang's personal prestige among the dissident elements played a significant role in their liberation through peaceful means.

National unity was Tsiang's political ideal, and he exercised a greater influence than anyone else in seeking the middle way in political disputes during the critical years. Probably this was his greatest service to his country, and unquestionably it was the one that was most expected of him. Had he lived until today, China's story might have been very different.

The importance of General Tsiang in the story of my religious journey, however, is that although he was not a Catholic, he preached Catholicism enthusiastically. Filial piety was at the bottom of this, no doubt. The tree is judged by its fruits. It was this spiritual gift of his, even more than the natural traits of his ardent personality, that finally, after his death, brought his wife and two daughters into the Church.*

He loved to talk, and it was a delight to hear him relate the history of Christianity in China. According to his account, it made its first appearance in the seventh century, in the reign of T'ang T'ai-tsung (627–649). During the Mongol rule in the thirteenth century, it became fairly widely extended in China proper. Among the outstanding Catholic missionaries was Archbishop John of Montecorvins, of the order of Friars Minor. Franciscan houses were established in several Chinese cities. Chiefly responsible for carrying the Faith into the interior was Father Metteo Ricci, an extraordinarily able and devoted Italian Jesuit who, by his skill in mathematics and astronomy and his knowledge of the Chinese classics, won the respect of the ruling scholar class. The benevolent attitude he adopted toward ancestral and Confucian cults, moreover, did much to ensure the success of his mission. Among the early Jesuit converts was Hsu Kuang-ch'i, a scholar-statesman, whose family village, Zikawei, on the outskirts of Shanghai, became the chief Christian center in China during the nineteenth and twentieth centuries.

In the eighteenth century, however, the Catholic Church fell upon evil days. Prolonged controversy

---

* Mrs. Tsiang was baptized by Reverend Father John T. S. Mao at Shanghai in 1947.

among missionaries over the propriety of the attitude taken by Ricci and his successors toward Chinese rites divided the Western representatives of the Faith. Powerful enemies profited by the division and succeeded in expelling the missionaries from China. Finally, in 1773, the Society of Jesus itself was suspended by the Pope and could therefore send no reinforcements. After this China was plunged into strict seclusion and remained almost unknown to the world at large for several generations.

During this spell of complete isolation, the arts, culture, and faith of the Chinese held their society in a rigid form. There was scarcely any introduction of science, machinery, or thought. In this connection, General Tsiang often expressed deep regret over the setback which the Catholic mission in China had suffered. He deplored the long-drawn-out quarrel over the rites, which by its spate of sterile passions and inept arguments had destroyed the splendid work undertaken with such vision by the early missionaries, and impeded the intellectual, scientific, and moral achievements which would have given strength and vitality to the Catholic apostolate, so desperately needed to bring about the regeneration of our society and our country.

From General Tsiang I derived immense intellectual stimulation, and his enthusiasm for Christian

civilization was communicated to me. Through him
I made the acquaintance of Archbishop Mario Zanin
at Hankow in March 1937, when he was the Apostolic
Delegate to China. The impression he made on me
was so deep that I can hardly forget him in my life.
He was a quiet, lighthearted priest, austere yet kindly,
dignified but easy-mannered, his whole personality
reflecting an inner discipline by which natural im-
pulses had been subordinated to the requirements of
Christian character. I had never seen anyone so calm,
so certain, and so peaceful in his absolute confidence
in God.

Again through General Tsiang I met Archbishop
Paul Yu Pin of Nanking, when we were in Rome in
October 1937 for a special mission. His dignity and
calm too inspired my immediate respect. I remember
how he answered me when I complimented him on
his outstanding qualities: "I do have one advantage
above other men. I am over six feet tall." He is a
priest big in every way: the bigness is not merely
physical: it comes from the Holy Ghost dwelling
constantly within him, and moving him in all that he
does. More than once I heard him say that priests do
not convert; they merely hoe the earth a little and
make the growing easier. Actually, he never fails to
show an ever clearer understanding of the needs of
the innumerable souls coming to him. His very appear-

ance is a sermon. Just to see him say Mass will make one concede that he is a man of God. To me he seems like a pencil with which God writes His name in the hearts of others, or a plow with which God breaks the stubborn soil in His field. My observation of him removed forever from my mind a certain dubiety I had had concerning Catholic priests, based on a misapprehension widespread among unbelievers: the notion that the Catholic Church uses all the wiles of the traveling salesman in order to ensnare the guileless.

I have already remarked that General Tsiang and I were in Rome in 1937 for a special mission. I cannot proceed without briefly recalling this mission and its purpose, even though it was a complete failure.

We arrived in Rome in October. We had been sent by our government to Italy for the special purpose of persuading the Fascist regime not to associate itself with Japan, and particularly not to participate in the so-called Anti-Comintern Pact, which had been concluded between Hitlerite Germany and Imperialist Japan in 1936. As both the Germans and the Japanese were at the time bringing increased pressure to bear upon Italy to form the Tripartite Pact, relations between Italy and China were acutely strained. We waited nearly two weeks without any response to our formal request for an interview with Mussolini.

On the 22nd of October, an official dinner party was given by General Tsiang in the Chinese Embassy* in honor of Professor de'Stefani upon the fulfillment of his mission in China. The Italian Cabinet and members of the Diplomatic Corps, with the exception of the representatives from the Axis Powers, were invited. As Minister of Foreign Affairs, Conte Ciano also was present. When the waiters had cleared the tables the doors were closed. General Tsiang stood up, grasping the back of his chair and smiling. He made a short, emphatic address. I venture to repeat here the words he used, which I had the pleasure of translating orally into Italian. They seemed to rise so naturally in his mind on the occasion and in the surroundings. "Upon my arrival here," he began, "one news agency reported that the main purpose of my trip is to buy arms and munitions. Yes, it is true! I have come here to buy arms and munitions!"

The words were received by the audience in astounded silence. Some of the Italian officials were visibly embarrassed. Most of the diplomats, while conceding that modern diplomacy should not wrap itself in mystery, were startled by the inappropriateness of such a public announcement. But then, in a changed tone, General Tsiang continued: "But the

* The Embassy was then headed by Ambassador Liu Von-tao, to whom I owe much for his guidance.

arms and munitions that I am hoping to secure are not visible but invisible, not material but spiritual!"

Here he was interrupted by loud applause. The audience had suddenly understood. After a short pause, he went on, musingly: " 'All roads lead to Rome.' Although this is a proverb of mediaeval times, I am convinced that it can still be applied today and in the long, infinite future."

In conclusion, General Tsiang said: "Justice and truth are two wings of spiritual force. They are to be found everywhere, and yet are secret. Invisible to the eye, impalpable to the senses, they are inherent in all things, and nothing can escape their operation. The world today is looking to the Eternal City for justice and truth, which have made it a strong moral force throughout the ages."

At the end of the dinner the facial expressions of the guests indicated that they had been much pleased by the General's address. The next day Ciano sent a request to the Chinese Embassy for a copy of the speech, and two days later we were received by Mussolini in the Palazzo Venezia.

It was late in the afternoon. General Tsiang dressed in full military uniform with decorations. I accompanied him as interpreter. As we entered the reception hall, which was also Mussolini's office, I saw Mussolini sitting before his writing table in the right-hand

corner. The room was vast. It seemed to me at least
40 x 80 feet. Mussolini rose and came to meet us half-
way. His face broke into a smile as he approached
us, but a rather artificial smile. Ciano appeared.
Mussolini took the General's hand. *"Come sta?"*
(How do you do?), he said. *"Siamo grati di averle."*
(We are glad to have you.)

We then proceeded together towards his table. We
were four; there were only two chairs. Mussolini
occupied one, the other was for General Tsiang. Ciano
and I stood.

The conversation began with General Tsiang's saying: "I am a soldier. In the name of the half million
Chinese warriors who have learned how to sacrifice
themselves for the salvation of their home country, I
feel much honored to be received by Your Excellency."

"This is Fascism!" Mussolini replied immediately,
without any hesitation.

General Tsiang shrugged slightly and continued:
"So far as material equipment is concerned, China
bears no comparison with Japan. Numerically the
odds are worse than ten to one. In terms of war
potential they are even one hundred to one. But the
Chinese have one weapon which our enemy does not
have. Sometimes this weapon is mislaid, sometimes it
breaks, but it is always found again and repaired.

That weapon is conviction—a wonderful, majestic belief in the cause of justice and independence, so strong that other men throughout the world can feel it too." There was a touch of defiance, though velvet-edged defiance, in his eyes as he said this.

When General Tsiang presented a case it was his practice to give illustrations, and he did so now. He leaned back against the chair and, with characteristic thoughtfulness, placed his words well: "It is not the ordinary person but the botanist who can easily distinguish between the sprouts of a palm and a cherry. The cherry tree blossoms, but the beauty is only temporary. The palm tree grows slowly, gives no fragrance, but its life is everlasting."

With a blunt finger he probed beneath the surface. "The Chinese people are much concerned about the talk in the press regarding the eventual participation of Italy in the Anti-Comintern Pact," and so saying he touched the point at issue. "Japan, like the cherry blossom, emblem of its national character, swiftly blossoming into riotous beauty but failing just as quickly, has used the Pact only as a mask for her imperialistic purposes in China. The Chinese people do not see any reason why Italy should even consider such a thought. The Psalmist has said: 'The just shall flourish like the palm tree: he shall grow up like the cedar of Libanus.' I hope that Your Excellency, as an experienced botanist in human relations, will make the right choice."

Mussolini had been leaning back in his chair. He gave the appearance of being not much interested in the discussion, but an irritable frown showed that he felt he had been caught. He was literally breathless for some seconds. He hesitated, then his forehead cleared as he suddenly sat up stiffly, planted his elbows firmly on the table, and tightened his lips into a grim, determined line. Looking straight at General Tsiang he said: "The participation of Italy in the Anti-Comintern Pact is unavoidable. The world today is divided into two fronts: the Anglo-American bloc and the Berlin-Rome Axis. When the former says 'yes' the latter has to say 'no' and vice-versa. Now Japan is against the Anglo-American bloc, and therefore is welcome to be our friend. If China stands up against the western imperialists we shall be only too happy to fall into line with your great country."

These words were Mussolini's final statement on the subject.

Before concluding the interview, General Tsiang presented Mussolini with a copy of the Chinese Encyclopedia in its abbreviated form, remarking that only a country as ancient and noble as Italy deserved to be the recipient of the gift which was a symbol of ancient Chinese culture. Mussolini accepted it with a faint smile. He opened the book and glanced at its content with an air of omniscience. He was, as a matter of fact, holding it upside down.

Ten days after our interview, Mussolini formally declared Italian participation in the Pact. His fate resulting from this decision could easily be anticipated in the light of what would surely have happened if he had decided otherwise.

Our mission had been a complete failure; or so, at least, I thought at the time. Personally I benefited from the visit from a religious point of view. First of all, I had learned from General Tsiang that a religious approach to political difficulties was high statesmanship. Secondly, the visit afforded me the opportunity of renewing and deepening my acquaintance with the Catholic art and history of Italy. During my various visits to the major Italian cities in addition to Rome, I came to know with some understanding the Catholic saints—St. Francis in Assisi, St. Catherine in Siena, St. John Bosco in Turin, St. Ambrose in Milan, St. Thomas Aquinas in Naples and St. Margaret of Cortona in Tuscany—and, what is more, the Holy House of Loreto, near Ancona, which, according to tradition, is Our Lady's house brought by angels to Loreto from Nazareth in the thirteenth century. It is now covered with rich marble and enshrined within a great basilica. And though I was unaware of it at the time, the noble personalities of these saints, their heroic spirit of detachment and conformation to Christ, were exercising a profound though subtle interior influence upon me, integrating the stirrings of religious impulse and slowly weaving a spiritual texture into my mind and my heart.

VII

Moral Re-Armament

*"Jesus said to them: Come
after me; and I will make you
to become fishers of men"
(Mark 1:17).*

Perhaps no one has expressed more succinctly the power of pain to purchase heaven than Schiller in these lines:

> "Millions, bravely sorrows bearing,
>   Suffer for a better time!
>   See, above the starry chime
>   God a great reward preparing!"

My own religious hunger was intensified by a spiritual vacuum resulting from the sorrowful loss of my wife.

After I returned to China from Italy in 1939 I served with the Ministry of Communications of the Chinese Government. Then I was appointed Deputy Director General of the National Highway Transportation Bureau, which also supervised transportation on the Burma Road, chief artery into China during World War II.

Most unfortunately it was at this time that my wife contracted a fatal disease which called for an emergency operation. We were all tired men in these days, suffering from a succession of continuous all-day bombings—twenty-two hours out of twenty-four. Relays of Japanese bombers in units varying from large squadrons to flights of a few planes were making savage attacks on Chungking, the War Capital of China. The difficulty of living conditions was extreme. Burdened with public duties, I was too absorbed to notice her failing health. Moreover, hospital facilities left much to be desired. When she was received for treatment her case was delayed and neglected, with fatal results. She died at the age of twenty-eight.

Things had obviously gone so wrong that I could not but point an accusing finger at myself. I could never escape my consciousness of negligence. I spent my days in the valley of sighs and mourning. A Chinese proverb says: "Blessings never come in pairs, misfortunes never happen singly." Only a few months after my wife's death my grandmother, who had loved me the most in my childhood, died in her ninety-third year, during the Japanese occupation of my native town. Cruel Japanese soldiers drove nails through her hands when she refused to satisfy their unjust and unreasonable demands. To my grandmother, a "secret Christian," as St. Augustine calls the devout pagan, this meant dying well; but it was like a knife plunged into my heart.

"I looked for one that would grieve together with me, but there was none: and for one that would comfort me, and I found none" (Ps. 68:21). In this mental, emotional, physical and spiritual suffering my soul, my whole nature, cried out for supernatural consolation. The source of my melancholy and grief went to the core of my being, and it could respond to no superficial remedy; something or someone was required to fill my great emptiness. This spiritual vacuum had an enormous part in my conversion, though I was often able to ignore it when I felt my pain a little relieved. Souls groping in the darkness find that grief gives man the opportunity to make Job's gift to God: the gift of trust in ultimate goodness, when he seems most to be the abject victim of evil. Then I came to understand why converts' pages are often blotted with tears. In fact those that sow in tears shall reap in joy. This is why Raoul Plus says: "Souls are won by words, won by example, but above all, they are won by sacrifice."

The immediate result of the loss of my wife and the heroic sacrifice of my beloved grandmother was a terrible inner numbness and a loss of equilibrium. The balance I had painfully achieved and long maintained was destroyed. I was like a ship without a

95

rudder, tossed about by every wind that blows. Grief, loneliness, despair took possession of my soul. Then came a conscious spiritual hunger, which continued to grow in me. In this regard I think that a passing reference to my wife's life would not be entirely out of place.

My wife was born in Shanghai. She was of fragile build and somewhat delicate in health. As a child she was shy and thoughtful above the average, but at the same time gracious and full of quiet fun. At an early age, and in spite of her natural shyness, she often went out of her way to make friends with various poor and aged people who lived near her home. At times she left with them a portion of her pocket money or a bit of candy. Her generous, tender little heart was fertile soil for the seed of sympathy and charity. A thoughtful helpfulness, a readiness, a willingness, even an eagerness, to do hard, disagreeable things— above all, for other people—constituted an outstanding trait in her character that manifested itself even more strongly in her maturer years.

I found her a true life's companion, exceedingly dear. She had not been brought up with any religious background. Nevertheless, her life had always been nourished by the love, simplicity and courage which were the well-springs of her nature. In this connection the memory of one incident is especially treasured.

It happened in August of 1937, during the outbreak of the Sino-Japanese War. I was tied up in Nanking. My wife and our two sons, George and Charles, were staying with my mother and two sisters in a little village, about twenty miles from our native town, as they considered it safer to take refuge there. One evening around seven o'clock, the usual time for them to go to bed, they heard someone knocking at the door. As they did not expect anyone to call at that time, they sensed trouble of some sort. My mother urged my wife to seek shelter with the rest of the family and leave her to face the danger alone, and my wife withdrew to another room.

As my mother opened the door two ruffians, one with a pistol in his hand, appeared before her. They demanded the delivery of my elder son, George, then six years of age, whom they wished to take as a hostage for ransom. My mother pretended that nobody was at home. The ruffians threatened her and demanded that she tell the truth. At this moment my wife suddenly reappeared and thrust herself as a shield before my mother. Her intervention had, of course, no weight with the attackers, but just as they were about to lay hands on her, rescue came. A servant from my native town called unexpectedly. Upon his arrival the ruffians took to their heels. The pistol they carried was a fake.

In retrospect, the secret of my wife's courage and

firmness of will seems to me to have been derived from more than natural endowments. In our ten years of life together she manifested a balance, a serenity and a mysterious wisdom which are typically the reward of the practice of supernatural virtues, and must in large measure be attributed to her profound understanding and practice of the Chinese ethic. I acknowledge in all honesty that for a long time she acted as a brake upon any inclination I had to act in defiance of good will and purity of heart, and go off the rails.

My passionate grief for the passing away of my wife and my grandmother was partly assuaged when I travelled for about one month, together with Mr. Chang Kia-ngau, then Minister of Communications, on a tour of inspection to the Northwest part of China. Mr. Chang encouraged me, shared with me the wisdom derived from his own experience, and told me that now Heaven wanted me to embrace duty whole-heartedly and be a real lover of our country. On returning I devoted my sorrowful heart to the problems of what was called "Stage-Transportation."

This was a very primitive kind of transportation, carried on by mules, horses, wheelbarrows, and human labor. It had been proved useful, and practical too, before roads were built and modern facilities of transportation employed. At the time, transportation on the Burma Road, the only link between the outside world and the interior of China, was disrupted. The desperate shortage of fuel had nearly paralyzed the whole structure of motor transport, producing damaging effects upon our military effort. In the face of this dangerous situation I strongly urged the immediate establishment of a nationwide "Stage-Transportation" system. And such a system did, in fact, come into being before very long. As a result, I was appointed Chairman of the Planning Board of the newly established National Stage-Transportation Administration. It is not my purpose here to go into the outstanding results derived from the employment of this primitive means of transportation; I only mention it because my wholehearted devotion to this most interesting work did much to relieve my depression at that time.

It was not until I married my present wife, in 1941, that I felt at all like myself again, however. She is my deceased wife's younger sister. Before this union took place, many friends kept me from marrying by suggesting motives for matrimony which considerably narrowed my choice of a wife: a wife with money, they said, could benefit my career; many great men, in the absence of love, had given themselves to the study of wisdom in the state of marriage.

Looking back, I am unable to find in myself the

power that drew my soul's vision out of that deep pit. It was only by the infinite mercy of God that I did not give way to inward infirmity. I finally entered into the marriage which replaced the earlier relationship so adequately that I was enabled to follow exactly the same patterns of conduct, and it was as if there had never been a spiritual wreck in my life. I cannot say, with the Vicar of Wakefield, "I chose my wife, as she chose her wedding gown, for qualities that would wear well." God's providence chose her for me.

I have been married to my present wife for ten years. This is no place to describe our courtship. I cannot, however, be content without telling what I have learned from her not only as wife, but as mother, partner, and fellow-worker. Although she is eight years younger than I, I have seen in her since the day of our marriage the commanding stature of a mother, an elder sister, an excellent teacher. This does not mean in the least that I am a Rip Van Winkle; but her maturity is greater than mine. She has had much to suffer from me, especially from my frequent loss of temper; but her quiet strength and patience, the deep unchanging wisdom in her heart, have again and again compelled my admiration. In short, her extraordinary love, and the singlemindedness with which she not only accepts cheerfully the day-to-day drudgery of kitchen and nursery and the inevitable evolution of married life, but moreover turns every-day troubles and crosses into joy, lead me to be conscious always of my family's dependence on me, and fill me with a determination to take care of them, provide for them and cherish them, cost what it may.

When I say that she keeps herself in constant gaiety, I do not mean that she is never moved to tears. But her tears are shed in secret, her griefs confided to herself alone. And more than any word could, the evidence of her tears moves my heart and leads me away from my vices, to face the reality of life. If I endeavor to find the source of the reverence in which I hold her, it may be traced to my early worship of the Chinese Goddess of Mercy, the great Küan Yin. It seems to me indeed that, even on a purely natural reckoning, her lips are the lips of a woman, but her smile is the smile of a living Küan Yin.

My spiritual poverty at the loss of my first wife and my grandmother and the extraordinary good fortune of my second marriage contributed each in its measure to my search for belief in a personal God and my recognition of the Godhead of Jesus once again—or would it be truer to say that now I began my first real search for Him? I argued that if God actually existed, and if He cared for me, then I had need of Him; and the fact that He did exist and did care for me seemed evidenced in my own life: I had been shattered and wonderfully restored. So I began to turn to Him, for my own advantage. But, as St. Thomas says: "From the fact that man hopes to obtain a benefit from God, he is led to think that God, his benefactor, is good in Himself. This is why hope disposes us to love God for Himself." * It was a combination of spiritual loneliness and a sense of gratitude that led me to approach the Oxford Group, which is also called "Moral Re-Armament" (MRA).

The first MRA friend whose acquaintance I made was an American and a pious Protestant. He was a radio commentator, and he was living at the Press Hostel in Chungking, where I lived. I delighted in his companionship. A kind of benevolence shone in his face, and his sincerity of heart gave a special flavor of joy to the pleasures we shared. But despite this friendship, Protestantism itself looked neither better nor worse to me than when I had first come across it. He did not mention MRA to me at first, as he had an inkling of my experience with Christianity at college. He supposed that if he talked to me about MRA I would show very little interest, and might even reject it completely as an old story.

One day, however, I was surprised to see his

---

* *Summa Theologica* Ia, IIae, q. 62, a. 4.

servant take a number of his belongings from his room, and I could not avoid finding out the reason. He told me quite frankly that his regular income did not defray his expenses, and he had, therefore, to make ends meet by pawning his personal effects. The explanation confused me the more since I had understood that his salary was on the basis of U.S. dollars. He should be able to afford a comfortable life, or at least get along without resorting to loans.

To explain his situation better, he showed me all the foreign exchange bills with the Central Bank of China for his income during the past two years. They were all exchanged according to the official rate, one U.S. dollar to twenty Chinese *Fa Pei*. Now the free market could offer about two thousand *Fa Pei* for one U.S. dollar, nearly one hundred times as much as one received from the bank according to the official rate, and dealing on the free market was by no means unusual, especially among foreigners. But he was hindered by a scruple of conscience.

His perfectly law-abiding spirit, absolute honesty and wholehearted appreciation of poverty erased my previous prejudice toward Christianity in its Protestant form. I was so much impressed that I now listened readily to his explanation of MRA.

The story of MRA is too well-known to need retelling here. The fact that MRA was initiated by Dr.

Frank Buchman, ably assisted by the late Bishop Logan Herbert Roots of the Protestant Episcopal Church, is common knowledge. Bishop Roots (1870–1945), a missionary in China for thirty-four years, possessed an unrivalled personal acquaintance with the leaders of modern China. He met Frank Buchman in Kuling, in 1917, and helped him to organize his first international gathering there the following year. Thus MRA is really of Chinese origin.

MRA's essential purposes are to establish a wholesome moral life in the home, the spirit of cooperation in industry, unity in the nation, and then peace in the world. I was first attracted by certain features it had in common with the teachings of Confucius. For example, MRA and Confucianism alike say we should love our neighbors. They both lay down an important rule: that a man should not pass judgment on the actions of another man without first passing judgment on his own.

MRA puts its spirit into practice by means of meditation and seeking providential guidance. Meditation is generally agreed to consist in the methodical consideration of a previously prepared subject, which has been divided into "points"; and in this way one is led to the production of a number of acts of "affections"—this is often called a colloquy—as well as to the formation of some practical resolution for one's

104

conduct. It amounts roughly to this, that a man must daily think of God and of his own relations with Him. In short, it is a kind of mental prayer, a silent inter-course of the soul with God, and it is to be regarded as constituting a training for the life of heaven, that will be nothing but an eternal, loving contemplation of the Godhead.

I need not dwell here upon the course of MRA, for whatever specific idea I may at the outset have had in my mind, my personal experience was such that MRA did not convert me; but it did chasten me and give me a view of my interior, spiritual weakness. Judging by human and natural standards, and within the limits of the intellectual order, I must acknowledge that MRA is a way leading to a certain psychological purity. However, considered as a religion, it is inade-quate in the absence of specific belief in God on the part of the practitioner; it is a concentration on the means without the object in view. Or so I found it. Without a clear and absolute belief in God's exist-ence, how can one experience His presence? The truth of the matter is that although I attended several MRA gatherings, my meditations were a failure; it was like trying to make fire without fuel. I can say from observation that my experience was not that of others in the Group whose spiritual foundations were firmer than mine, and I have never lost my admiration for

MRA, but the fact remains that although it was a favorable current in my spiritual navigation, its influence was but temporary; it left me still groping.

VIII

All Roads to Rome

"I am the way, and the truth, and the life. No man cometh to the Father, but by me" (John 14:6).

I began my career as a young diplomat when I was appointed Adviser to the Chinese Delegation to the Council of Foreign Ministers held at Lancaster House, London, in September and October 1945. Immediately after the Council's meeting I was assigned as Chargé d'Affaires with ministerial rank at the Chinese Embassy in Rome. This was my third visit to Italy. All my memories of this lovable, religious country were renewed in my heart, and I had a deep sense of happiness.

Rome and Italy cannot be all things to all people, but to me Rome is the place where I find the sun not only in the sky, as it is in the rest of Italy, but in the hearts of the people. Rome spells peace, which is what I want above all else. But a peace without isolation, which I abhor. I want to have peace in the midst of many people, and here I find it. All roads lead to

109

Rome. Rome, the city founded upon Seven Hills, dominant in human history for 2,500 years, has an atmosphere impossible to describe; in it light and shadow, the vivid present and the nostalgic past, abundant life and the record of life in stone, are blended into a curious unity which gives it a charm above that of other great cities. But what is unique is the sense one has of being somehow in touch with a kind of collective memory in which the experience of the Catholic faith from antiquity is preserved in its historical reality.

The Chinese Embassy in Rome had been closed down during the war. My first duty was to reopen it and to seek a suitable official residence. It happened that a villa of real architectural beauty, which had been originally built for Mussolini, was still not let. With the assistance of the Italian Government, I was able to lease it. However, there was a delicate matter to be dealt with: there were about forty nuns staying on the premises, and the lessee himself must find some means of getting them to leave.

I had an instinctive respect for nuns, originating perhaps in my early admiration of Küan Yin. But something I read in *The Autobiography of Benjamin Franklin* no doubt had some bearing in my view. The passage is the following:

In a garret of her house there lived a maiden lady of seventy, in the most retired manner, of whom my landlady gave me this account: that she was a Roman Catholic, had been sent abroad when young, and lodged in a nunnery with the intent of becoming a nun; but, the country not agreeing with her, she returned to England, where, there being no nunnery, she had vowed to lead the life of a nun, as near as might be done in those circumstances. Accordingly, she had given all her estate to charitable uses, reserving only twelve pounds a year to live on, and out of this sum she still gave a great deal in charity, living herself on water-gruel only, and using no fire but to boil it. She had lived many years in that garret, being permitted to remain there gratis by successive Catholic tenants of the house below, as they deemed it a blessing to have her there. A priest visited her to confess her every day. "I have asked her," says my landlady, "how she, as she lived, could possibly find so much employment for a confessor." "Oh," said she, "it is impossible to avoid *vain thoughts.*" I was permitted once to visit her. She was cheerful and polite, conversed pleasantly. The room was clean, but had no other furniture than a mattress, a table with a crucifix and book, a stool which she gave me to sit on, and a picture over the chimney of Saint Veronica displaying her handkerchief, with the miraculous figure of Christ's bleeding face on it, which she explained to me with great seriousness. She looked pale, but was never sick; and I give it as another instance on how small an income, life and health may be supported.*

---

* Pocket Book Edition, New York, p. 55.

This, for me, had been more than a report of an event. It had given me a vivid insight concerning the spirituality of a person who sees God in everything and everything in God, and filled me with wonder.

Although I anticipated that no difficulty would arise with the nuns, my inner esteem for them was so strong that it seemed hardly possible to mention the matter of vacating the house to them. However, the Embassy was in urgent need of a residence, and owing to the extreme shortage of housing in Rome I could not find any other place suitable. I saw that I must put the question to them in person.

My first visit to them gave me an opportunity to observe at close range their well-ordered, ascetic life. In spite of the fact that I had already learned something about the little sacrifices practised by a nun—in food, in drink, in labor, in watching, in posture, in all the little details of life—I could not help being amazed at the stubborn generosity the sacrifices and trials of these sisters must have demanded.

Winters are severe in Rome, and the chill November wind rioted at will through the vast, marble building. Although there were many rooms available, the nuns all stayed in the reception room on the ground floor, which was the coldest spot in the house. My immediate impression was that this was an industrious, serious community of women ardently devoted to an

austere ideal; living in dire poverty and great peace.
They sat there praying and shivering, but apparently
declining to put on any mantles; at most shrinking
against a blast of especial bitterness. (I learned later
that they never had any extra mantles.) The room they
occupied served as dormitory, refectory, scriptorium,
chapter room, and chapel for daily prayer and contemplation. They simply slept with their straw mat-
tresses on the bare floor, with sacks of stalks for
pillows. As I looked at the bare refectory, with its
line of earthenware water jugs and its wooden spoons,
I learned how little the nuns got to eat: only a few
vegetables and some bread and, once in a while, milk
and cheese. Almost everything they had was broken,
except their Rule.

If I had known anything then about the habits worn
by the various religious orders, I should have recognized their black cloaks and robes as belonging to
the Benedictines. So deeply impressed was I by their
spirituality and holiness of life that I was holding
myself in readiness to retreat if my request produced
any objection. However, they listened cheerfully and
expressed their willingness to leave the building on
condition that their convent, which was being occupied
by a certain military organization belonging to Allied
Occupation Forces, be returned to them. They had
tried every conceivable method to get it back, but

their efforts had been met with cold indifference. Unless their residence was returned to them, they had practically nowhere to go.

The desire to secure the prompt return of the convent to the nuns seized me so strongly that my plan for taking over the building for the use of my Embassy was almost forgotten, although of course the questions were related. I took up the matter immediately with the competent Allied authorities in Rome. Thanks to the assistance of the American Ambassador, Mr. Alexander Kirk, and the American General Brown, then Commander-in-Chief of the Allied Occupation Forces, the whole affair was settled within three days. The Allied military organization was evacuated from the convent, the nuns returned happily to their proper sanctuary after an absence of several years, and I soon took possession of the villa and established official residence there. Everything had gone more smoothly than could ever have been imagined.

In relating this story I wish to point out that although at the time in my heart I received a deep impression of the supernatural gladness, lightheartedness, and felicity of these nuns, I scarcely understood it. How could they manage to nourish their interior life under such living conditions? How could it be that the huge, draughty building, comparable in temperature to the frigidity of Dante's lowest pit, should house the happiest people in the world? Only since I have found myself in the Church do I understand the freedom from care which arises from complete dependence upon God.

Before concluding this chapter I must mention another occasion on which I was conscious of God's providence disposing all things well.

During my term of office in Rome I was often much affected by the miseries I observed among my fellow-countrymen residing in Italy. There were in particular forty Chinese, former employees of the Lloyd Triestino Shipping Company, who were in dire need. During the war they had been interned in an Italian concentration camp, and now, since the shipping company did not function after the end of hostilities, they were without employment, living from hand to mouth.

Since all questions outstanding between China and Italy were being reserved for settlement with the conclusion of the Peace Treaty, a diplomatic approach to the problem did not seem feasible. The plight of these men kept me always in a state of uneasiness.

In February 1946 Bishop Tien of Tsingtao was elevated to the Cardinalate, the first of our race to be so honored. He came to Rome to receive the Red Hat and I, on the instructions of my Government, gave an official dinner party in his honor. That evening the question of the forty Chinese shipping employees was uppermost in my mind, and in the presence of the Cardinal, I discussed it with another of my guests, Admiral de Curton, then Italian Minister of the Navy —he also had jurisdiction over mercantile navigation, but I did not discover this until later on. To my surprise and pleasure, he said that immediate action should be taken and asked me to send him a memorandum of the matter.

Naturally I lost no time in following the Admiral's instructions. A week later the whole question was settled to the satisfaction of all parties. A certain sum was paid by the Ministry of the Navy on behalf of the shipping company. Within a month these forty men happily rejoined their families at Shanghai by a special arrangement of the Italian transport authorities.

Now anyone who finds nothing remarkable in this incident simply does not realize the amount of red-tape a diplomat must go through in trying to deal with a government on behalf of individuals. I cannot think that my personal influence could have had any tangible effect on the situation without the precise combination of events that brought the Cardinal, the Minister of the Navy, and myself together to discuss the question. All coincidence, you say? That may be, but my interpretation of it is this: when God is trying to teach us to rely on Him, instead of trusting in our own strength, sometimes He produces just such a "coincidence" to show us how simply things can be done with His help.

IX

Dr. Wu

"We know that to them that love God all things work together unto good: to such as, according to his purpose, are called to be saints" (Rom. 8:28).

In July 1946 I was in Paris, serving as Adviser to the Chinese Delegation to the Peace Conference. It was not even a conference of compromise, much less a conference of peace. Can there be any true peace for men, when they are deaf to the word of God? I cannot pretend I recognized then that in the whole universe there is only one Peacemaker, namely, Christ. But I was deeply conscious of the ineffectuality of man-made plans in face of the force of evil in the world.

After the conference of no peace, I returned to my original post in Rome, and now my attraction to the Church was growing at about the same rate as the world was sickening and failing. How is it explicable that a man so strongly attracted to the Church as I was could still remain outside it, could not see it from

121

inside, but only from the visitors' gallery? Here a passage from Chesterton is of some relevance to my condition:

The truth of the Catholic Church is like a magnet with powers of attraction and of repulsion. The repulsion arises from the vague fear that one may be caught in a baited trap; but the bait is simply the truth. The moment men cease to pull against the Catholic Church, they feel a tug toward it. The moment they cease to shout it down they begin to listen to it with pleasure. The moment they try to be fair to it they begin to be fond of it. But when that affection has passed a certain point it begins to take on the tragic and menacing grandeur of a great love affair.*

My falling in love with Christ took place at the time of my appointment as Deputy Delegate to the Chinese Delegation to the United Nations Investigation Commission on Greece in January 1947, and it is more to the matchmaker, Dr. John C. H. Wu, than to anyone else that I owe the attainment of my holy marriage.

Before I left for Greece, Dr. Wu, then Chinese Minister to Vatican City, gave me a copy of the Chinese version of the Psalms translated by himself. I had learned the Psalms and sung them when I studied

_____

* *The Catholic Church and Conversion* (Macmillan), pp. 61–62.

at the Methodist College, yet without appreciation. Now when I came to read the Chinese version, its wisdom, beauty and dignity seemed to exceed anything in literature, poetry or philosophy.* My heart became immersed in it like a sponge in the sea. It was in this book that I was thus engrossed when an incident occurred which I shall never forget.

The date was February 22, 1947. In the company of Ambassador Wunsz King I was on a flight between Athens and Salonika. When the Skymaster took off that morning, the weather had seemed perfect for flying, but after forty minutes in the air, we ran into storm conditions and were told that the plane could not land at Salonika but must return to Athens. On the trip back, the weather grew steadily worse. The clouds were so thick and the wind so violent that the plane went off its course. To add to our difficulties, the plane's radio equipment, including the radio compass, "went out." As the weather prevented normal

---

* Only the Chinese version can satisfy the Chinese-speaking reader, and Dr. Wu's translation is, in my opinion, far the best for the average Chinese reader yet produced. This is rather remarkable, since Dr. Wu seldom writes poetry, especially Chinese poetry; but his translation of the psalms, in poetic form, reveals in him a rare power over words in their atmospheric and emotional content. His version abounds in beautiful lyrics that rise in the mind like music.

navigation and without a radio compass the pilot was unable to guide the plane, he had to cruise about for several hours, hoping against hope that some high point of land would become visible through the occasional breaks in the clouds. More terrible still, we were running short of fuel. Of course, no SOS could be dispatched. At this point the pilot thought it advisable to inform us fully concerning our prospects, and they were these: Eventually we should have to land in the sea; if the plane did not crack up on contact with the water, there would possibly be an interval of one or two minutes for us to get out before it sank. No "ditching" or survival equipment was available, except a few sets of life-belts. As no one on board seemed to be trained in this art of "ditching," the success of the venture was most doubtful.

We were told to watch the pilot for a signal. If he should point his thumb downwards, it would mean that the plane was going to "ditch" into the water; everything movable should then be jettisoned, the doors of all escape hatches should be opened, and everyone should prepare to leap out into the struggle for survival.

Altogether there were twenty-two persons on board. Next to me sat Ambassador King. We were, as I have said, reading the Chinese version of the Psalms. So engrossed were we in the book that our circumstances troubled us less than they should. The words of Job kept repeating themselves in my thought: "Although He should kill me, I will trust in Him" (13:15). Whether it was sheer trust in God's protection or the buoyant optimism natural to the Ambassador which affected us both, I do not know; probably it was a combination of both. At any rate we did not pay much attention to what was going on. We continued reading the Psalms and did not fully realize the seriousness of the situation—that it was a case of life or death—until we were assigned to the same window in case the signal should come to jump

"You are young and have a longer future than I; you go out the window first. Don't worry about me," said Ambassador King.

"No, you should jump first," I protested, "because you are older than I. I think I can resist longer, so I should come after."

After this exchange of courtesy about the order of jumping we both prudently untied our shoelaces in preparation for any eventuality and then returned to our reading. The Psalm happened to be the 44th:

"God is a refuge and a strength unto us; he has greatly shown Himself a help in times of trouble.

Therefore we fear not, while the earth is overthrown and the mountains fall into the midst of the sea.

Let its water rage and foam, let the mountains be
shaken by its might.

The Lord of hosts is with us; the God of Jacob is a
stronghold unto us."*

Meantime, although I had only a slight foundation
in spirituality and did not even know how to pray,
the need for prayer, for union with God, became a
hunger searching to the roots of my being. Unable to
understand my impotency, I nevertheless remained at
peace. Though I thought myself incapable of prayer,
I nevertheless prayed fervently that the forced landing
need not occur. To some extent Abraham Lincoln's
words about prayer represented my feeling: "I have
been driven many times to my knees by the overwhelming conviction that I had nowhere else to go;
my own wisdom and that of all around me seemed
insufficient for that day." However, there was another
factor. I was remembering a dream I had had the
night before. I had told Ambassador King and our
friends about it in the tearoom of the Hessani Airport
just before we took off. I had dreamt of traveling by
air with a group of colleagues, which included the
Ambassador. On the trip we made a forced landing,

* Reprinted from *The Psalms: A Prayer Book*, with the
permission of Benziger Brothers, Inc., publishers and copy-
right owners.

but no one was hurt. After the accident, the passengers took a bus back to their starting place.

At the time, my friends had taken little notice. The flight to Salonika was short; the weather was fine; no one thought of anything so unpleasant as a forced landing. But the dream had greatly impressed me. It seemed to me like a warning and an assurance from Our Lord concerning a trial to come; He would be with me and I had nothing to fear.

After a few more minutes flying, the pilot appeared with his thumb pointed *up*, indicating that he had sighted land! Presently we came down on a high piece of ground. As we descended we heard a tremendous noise like the beating of drums—a sign that the fuel tank was completely empty! The plane touched ground, then jumped like a skittish horse. We should all have gone straight through the roof had there been an opening. But actually no one was hurt.

As we left the plane the pilot remarked, "I never felt so relieved in my life as when I landed you safely in this place." Another two hundred yards of flying would have ended in catastrophe, he told us. He also said that he had been on the point of turning off the switch and diving into the water, when suddenly he decided to have one last try. It might be that the cloud right ahead of him hid land. He made the effort, and

127

as the result of his decision our lives were spared. We took a bus back to Athens.

Of course, that this last-minute decision by the pilot, which saved twenty-two lives, was made in response to prayer is the kind of thing we can never prove. But it needs no proof for me. I am convinced that God did intervene, that our escape was a sure indication of Divine protection.

The plane incident was an important factor in my advance toward the Christian life, for it made me conscious of my own poverty. It left me with a sense of the *need* of grace, of God's help, the need for adoration and prayer. Without these there is no beginning of the good life, no progress, no arriving at eternal salvation. This is a paradox, but before one recognizes God's presence, how can one really come to the Church "seeking Him"?

In her delightful book, *It's Greek to Me,* Mrs. Wille S. Ethridge * gives a vivid and detailed account of the U. N. Commission's life in Greece. She kindly refers to me as "The Holy Sih." I cannot trace the origin of this honorable title. Possibly, my devoted reading of the Psalms in the plane might have something to do with it.

---

* Mrs. Ethridge is the wife of Mark Ethridge, publisher of the *Louisville Courier-Journal* and the *Louisville Times* and Chief Delegate of the American Delegation on the U.N. Commission to Greece.

My work in Greece lasted only five months. During this period I had several opportunities to go to Rome. This made it possible for me to keep in touch with Dr. Wu. Our relationship became closer and more intimate. In retrospect I see this as another grace, renewing my spiritual energy in the journey toward God. St. Francis de Sales says: "If thou wouldst walk in earnest toward devotion, find some good man to conduct and guide thee." I found this man in Dr. Wu.

Concerning the character of Dr. Wu I can not do better than to borrow the words of Mr. F. J. Sheed, who says, in his introduction to Dr. Wu's remarkable autobiography *Beyond East and West:* "He is totally Catholic, totally Chinese, and totally himself." As the reader will perhaps remember, I made Dr. Wu's acquaintance when I was studying at the Comparative Law School of China, Soochow University, in 1928. He was its President and also my professor of Jurisprudence. He used to call himself, jokingly, "Doctor of Jurisimprudence." The fact is that the keenest of his students even then had some suspicion that his imprudence came from a higher prudence.

When I met him again, years later, he retained only one impression of me. He had asked in class one day, "What is law?" and I had replied, "Law is law." Though he had then launched into an illuminating discussion of the various meanings of law—its origin, its capacities, and its limits, its ends and aims, the purpose of its institution—he nevertheless considered that, from the point of view of the law of identity, my answer had not really been as laughable as might be supposed. To the astonishment of myself and my classmates, instead of censuring me, he praised me for the exactness and simplicity of my definition. I am sure that the whole class, myself included, had thought that he must be either a fool or a philosopher.

I often think with amusement and some embarrassment how unperceptive we boys were. I am reminded of the schoolfellows of St. Thomas who were deceived by his appearance of stolidity into calling him the "Dumb Ox"! Actually, Dr. Wu's occasional solemnity arises from simplicity, a spiritual quality; he is quite without coldness and has an excellent sense of humor. I must be pardoned for this panegyric, for I am only one of many students who entertain so much love and reverence for this eminent scholar. A successful lawyer, master of the principles, ideals and techniques of Anglo-American as well as Chinese law, he is tremendously respected as one of the most creative thinkers among Chinese jurists. When I came across the words of Judge Cuthbert W. Pound: "The judge should no doubt, like our own great Chief Judge, be both lawyer and philosopher of the highest grade, blessed with saving common sense and practical experience as well as sound and comprehensive learning,"* my immediate thought was: Dr. Wu.

In Rome I had the privilege of observing his way of life at close range, and it struck me that, if not full of contradictions, it was at least very different from that of ordinary people. The Legation provided him with a beautiful Oldsmobile, but he preferred walking, stick in hand. A number of servants were at his disposal, but he chose to make his tea with his own hands. Insects, he admitted, were a nuisance, but he would never agree to the use of exterminators, since, he pointed out, the insects were, after all, creatures of God, like ourselves. I never heard him complain of his political fortunes, although it was obvious that, with his talents and political experience, he was entitled to hold a far more advantageous position, in the worldly sense, than was represented by his post as emissary to the Holy See. He was never unhappy over finances, although his heavy financial burdens put his budget very often "in the red." I wonder whether he had any budget, as a matter of fact. He never seemed more joyful than when some trial had come to him. He was "as needy, yet enriching many."

One day, for example, I caught him off-guard in his

---

* Bulletin, New York State Bar Association, 1929, 285.

bedroom. He was somersaulting on the floor, and with each somersault he exclaimed, "O Father, you are too good! O Mother, you are too sweet!" The first thought which came to my mind was that he must have had some encouraging news. But as I was about to present my congratulations, he told me he had just received some little crosses; nothing gave him as much joy as little crosses did. How like Francis of Assisi he is, I thought; otherwise he would go mad. This revealing incident led me to further investigation of his Christian faith.

Dr. Wu used to hear Mass every morning at St. Agnes Church, which was within walking distance of his residence, Villa Blanc. Once he asked me to accompany him to a church and I did so. There I observed that, like St. John, resting his head on the heart of Christ, he prayed as earnestly as if he were calling God or one of His saints on the telephone. The thought came to me that although he loved both prayer and books, he must have learned more in prayer at the foot of the crucifix or near the tabernacle than in the most learned works. This is still my feeling about him.

Dr. Wu is a daily communicant. His practice of constant prayer sometimes gives him a distracted air. More than once in these days I met him and was scarcely noticed. He walked rapidly and with a decided stoop, giving the impression of being in a hurry to get somewhere—to church, no doubt. When he was interrupted, he was most polite, more apologetic than the apologizer. This did not suggest that he was rather happier when he was not interrupted. He was ready to leave his meditations at a moment's notice, but it seemed to me that when he resumed them, he walked all the faster. Externals suggested an internal condition to me—even then I thought that his contemplative life was a curiously active one. Contemplative or active, he usually remained in church for an hour or two before returning home for breakfast. His cook used to complain that he never knew how many there would be for this meal, or for lunch. The trouble was that Wu himself never knew how many people he would meet in church or on his way home.

Whenever I was upset over anything, he would say casually, "Don't worry. I offered up my Communion for you this morning." Or "I'll remember to ask the Little Flower to help you out!" I never said much more than "Umm" to any of this, as I did not even understand what Communion was or what the "Little Flower" might be, and he never expected more from me. I learned only later that when he said he would "remember me at Mass" he was actually praying for my soul.

Whenever I had time I liked to go to Dr. Wu's house, which I looked upon more as a home than a school or a library. Truly the atmosphere there was fragrant with Christian virtues. Pleasures that cost anything were infrequent, but all the more enjoyed, it seemed, because of the austerities resulting from the Wus' limited means. Ordinarily, in a large family such as this, there is some germ that tends to breed discord and confusion, but in the Wu household the bond between the members could have been only one of real love, for in this healthful atmosphere no germ could prosper.

I have come to understand that the Church is the outer wall of the castle, the home is the citadel, the sacred shrine, the inner sanctuary, where His love is best reflected. When men love one another and live together without fuss, willing to see things in the same light, to sacrifice their limited pleasures and to give up their own interests out of love for one another—then the Spirit of God is working among them, and His presence is most vividly felt in the mutual love, domestic peace and real unity. It is incomparable; it is beyond the reach of human nature alone. *Congregavit nos in unum Christi amor*—the love of Christ has brought us together.

It will be seen that whatever my love of God, I have never been lacking in the love of Wus! But this is to anticipate. I only knew then that I found the Wu family life attractive above all others.

X

"The Science of Love"

"Nor height, nor depth, nor any other creature, shall be able to separate us from the love of God which is in Christ Jesus our Lord" (Rom. 8:39).

The Rosary had an essential place in Wu's household. Often when I was there in the evening, I saw Dr. Wu gather his whole family together before retiring, to kneel down with their beads. Before each decade of Hail Marys, the Mystery was announced— Joyful, Sorrowful, Glorious, according to the day, recalling the events of the Savior's childhood, His sorrowful passion, His resurrection and ascension. I watched the Wus as the beads moved through their fingers, and although I was wholly uninstructed in this devotion, it was clear to me that here was no mechanical way of saying prayers but a kind of living meditation, which must penetrate more and more deeply into the mind and heart. The oftener I heard this recitation, the more it attracted me. I felt that it was somehow so close to human life, so spontaneous an ex-

pression of the heart, that I could not help joining
the party saying the prayers, even though I had not
learned any of them at the time.

Dr. Wu is essentially a philosopher and theologian
and has the habits of a scholar; yet his home was
always full of people. No one with whom I am acquainted, in public or private life, is more aware
of God's place in relation to his life and work than he.
For him, a personal knowledge of Christ is not a thing
to be folded away and secretly treasured: it is something to be put to work for others. In his own words,
"The best way to keep an experience of Christ is to
pass it on." How I felt then can only be described in
St. Augustine's words about Bishop Ambrose:

That man of God received me as a father, and as
bishop welcomed my coming. I came to love him, not
at first as a teacher of the truth, which I had utterly
despaired of finding in Your church, but for his kind-
ness towards me. I attended carefully when he
preached to the people, not with the right intention,
but only to judge whether his eloquence was equal to
his fame or whether it flowed higher or lower than
had been told me. His words I listened to with the
greatest care; his matter I held quite unworthy of
attention. I enjoyed the charm of his speaking,
though for all his learning it was not so pleasing and
captivating as that of Faustus. . . . But salvation is
far from sinners, of the sort that I then was. Yet

138

little by little I was drawing closer, though I did not yet realize it.*

It is impossible to describe Dr. Wu without discussing Madame Wu, for those who know them best say that her virtues are reflected in her husband, especially her patient persistence and unwavering devotion to the spiritual ideals close to her heart. It is an observable fact in China that priests make converts, but good Christian mothers make Christians. "Home is where Mother is." Heaven is where God is. When the mother of the family is a good Christian, the consequences are great. In this case, my wife was converted by Mrs. Wu's influence.

The first thing about Mrs. Wu which struck both my wife and myself as being specifically Christian was the fact that although, as the mother of thirteen children, she might have been expected to carry a considerable burden of care, yet she managed all her household duties with serenity and simplicity. Once my wife remarked to me privately that Mrs. Wu must have some secret of happiness. I understood then her heart must have been captivated by Mrs. Wu's virtues.

What this secret was, was clearly revealed to my wife when she asked Mrs. Wu directly, "Do you find it very difficult to be the mother of thirteen children

---

* *The Confessions of St. Augustine*, Bk. V; translated by F. J. Sheed.

and the wife of a diplomat who is also a spiritual writer?"

"No—it is nothing," Mrs. Wu gestured lightly. "His is the responsibility. 'My teacher' is dedicated to his work. I keep my place in the background. But I am always there when he needs me. I think a wife's function is not to complicate her husband's life, but to keep it calm and peaceful. Especially when his work is so demanding of his time and energies as 'my teacher's' is." (I need not point out how beautiful it was to hear her refer always to Dr. Wu as "my teacher," never by the more dignified titles by which he is known to others—Dr. Wu or Minister Wu.)

Never for a moment had Mrs. Wu implied that she was a religious woman. But is it not manifest in her conduct that to her "woman is meant to find her vocation as mother of man, and her share in the universal motherhood of Mary." * And does not her answer also describe the vocation of a woman according to the New Testament?

"Your beauty must lie, not in braided hair, not in gold trinkets, not in the dress you wear, but in the hidden features of your hearts, in a possession you can never lose, that of a calm and tranquil spirit; to God's eyes, beyond price. It was thus that the holy

---

* Gerald Vann, *Eve and the Gryphon* (Newman), p. 32.

women of old time adorned themselves, those women who had such trust in God, and paid their husbands such respect. Think how obedient Sara was to Abraham, how she called him her lord; if you would prove yourselves her children, live honestly, and let no anxious thoughts disturb you" (I Peter 3:4–6).

After this conversation my wife said to me that if it was the Christian spirit that led Mrs. Wu to such a degree of interior purity, selflessness, and perfect sincerity, she would count herself fortunate to be a Christian. Although she did not enter the Church until she was baptized with me about two years later, she has been a Catholic in spirit ever since the time of that conversation.

Before concluding this chapter, I must say something about my personal experience in the matter of Catholic reading inspired by Dr. Wu. My association with him broadened my intellectual interests considerably. It also intensified my love of learning. He lavished every care on my spiritual development, and whenever we met he would give me some Catholic books to read, which I would proceed to devour with avidity. But I borrowed many books on general subjects from his shelves and (I think somewhat to his surprise) the two volumes of *The Teaching of the Catholic Church*, by Canon G. D. Smith. Most of the books I took home were hardly opened, but they were there, at any rate, in case I needed something to read.

At about this time Dr. Wu's version of the New Testament came out, and since I had so much enjoyed his Psalms, he was kind enough to let me read the proofs of the new book before publication. Again I was deeply moved by the beauty of the Gospels in the Chinese language, and much of their substance remained in my mind, little as I realized it.* But there was another book that I read and reread many times. This was Dr. Wu's own *The Science of Love*.

To read this book is a pleasure. The author's personality shines through it full of ease and grace, wit and gentle satire. But beneath his apparent gaiety is the serious aim to win other souls to do as he did— join the Catholic Church.

The striking feature of the book is Dr. Wu's devotion to Saint Thérèse of Lisieux and her "Little Way." Now at last I came to understand what his references to "The Little Flower" meant. I felt closer to the saint when I learned from the book that in 1927 this little Carmelite Sister had cured Dr. Wu's daughter Lan-hsien of a very serious case of pneumonia. I was

---

* As in the case of the Psalms, Dr. Wu has succeeded most admirably in his translation of the New Testament. Especially the Epistles of St. Paul take on a new, clear meaning. The language is the Chinese of Han Yu and Liang Chi-chao —literary but modern, smooth and rhythmical.

further introduced to the "Little Way" itself. As Dr. Wu puts it: "The true Catholic conception of life is not, as it is sometimes falsely represented, a mere bargain with God, or a dry series of 'don'ts' with heavy sanctions, but a simple, complete and loving surrender of the creature to its Creator, a falling in love of man with God, and a kiss for a kiss, or rather a small kiss for a big kiss between the soul and its Redeemer."

This book of Dr. Wu's led me to read another, the *Autobiography of Saint Thérèse of Lisieux*. The reading of the little Carmelite's autobiography put me into a state of great excitement. What an exquisite miniature of spiritual perfection she was—a "miracle of virtues and a prodigy of miracles" as Pope Pius XI called her. I experienced a peculiar happiness as she told of her innumerable experiences in finding joy and sweetness in all that is bitter. When I came to read the words: "My spiritual aridity increased and I found no comfort in Heaven or on earth; yet amid these waters of tribulation so eagerly thirsted for, I was the happiest of mortals," * I could not help believing that in her life on earth she had already begun to live the life of the Blessed in Heaven. It seemed to me that all suffering had become her treasure. Truly,

---

* Edited by T. N. Taylor (Kenedy).

she traced for man the simple road which leads to great heights.

I put my whole heart into the reading of this book. Every word of it seemed the echo of my own inmost thoughts. The more I studied it, the more it fascinated me. It not only encouraged me to look for joy in trials but revealed to me the steady ascent that follows for those who thus accept suffering. But the experience amounted to more than the gracious influence of a book; I went on to learn as much as I could of the virtues of the saint herself, and I believe that she interceded for me, redoubling my love for our Mother, the Blessed Virgin. For is not the whole life of Thérèse like a reflected smile of Mary? I wonder very much how Protestantism can have so ignored devotion to the Blessed Virgin, who is the Mother of Christ and our own Mother?

If these recollections give the impression that my intellectual comprehension was such as to make it easy for me to become a Catholic, it must be borne in mind that God's revelation enters through the heart. Even at the Crucifixion it was Our Lord's purpose to leave us in such balanced uncertainty that belief in His divinity still required an effort of faith; and faith is not in the understanding alone, nor in the instincts; it is also in the will. The intellect presents the target, but the will shoots the arrows. The

Faith cannot be embraced except by an act of the will to which the intellect gives fully conscious approval; and it is moreover an act of will that implicates the whole personality. I was, in fact, neither able nor willing to take the step; and I had still very far to go before I should receive the power from God: "This people honoreth me with their lips: but their heart is far from me" (Matt. 15:8).

XI

Jekyll and Hyde

"Who crying to their companions say: we have piped to you, and you have not danced: we have lamented, and you have not mourned" (Matt. 11:17).

Although it is outside the scope of this book to go into a detailed history of the U. N. Commission's work in Greece, a brief account of the background of our mission seems not entirely irrelevant.

The problem of Greece came before the U. N. Security Council in 1946 when the Greek Government charged that the guerrilla movement in Greece was receiving substantial support from Albania, Bulgaria, and Yugoslavia. The U. N. Security Council, by unanimous decision, voted to establish a Commission of Investigation to examine the facts and to report concerning the troubled situation along the northern Greek frontiers. The Commission of Investigation, composed of representatives of the eleven members of the Security Council, spent several months in-

vestigating the situation, ascertaining the facts, studying the evidence, preparing its Report, and assisting members of the Security Council in their attempt
to find a solution of the problem. The work had no
substantial result, but this was more or less to be
expected in consideration of the participants themselves and the fact that the affair was handled by the
Security Council: the power of the Veto is self-
explanatory.

However, my own assignment on the Commission
was a very happy one. I shall ever retain a vivid
picture of my vigorous, enthusiastic, friendly, im-
petuous colleagues, spreading their sleeping-bags on
the ground under the soughing branches of the
Olympos mountain forests. Despite the doubtful outcome of their work, they devoted themselves whole-
heartedly to it for the cause of peace. Although the
Chinese Delegation was understaffed, and this put
a great strain upon me, I was still able to employ the
time not spent at meetings and on trips to good
advantage in seeing many famous Grecian ruins.

Greece is a stark, rock-ribbed promontory, excit-
ingly beautiful but not fertile, offering no invitation
to a life of self-indulgence. Life here is, and always
has been, tumultuous, a relentless struggle. When I
arrived in Athens my eyes lighted at once on the
Parthenon, the temple of Athena on the Acropolis. Its

serene, uncrumbling columns—pure white once, but burned to a soft gold by centuries of sun—are eloquent of how time and the hand of man have united to create the world's most beautiful piece of architecture. Seen by the light of a full moon, it looks like something rising out of another world. As I looked at it there came to my mind what St. Paul said before the Areopagus: "Men of Athens, whenever I look I find you scrupulously religious. Why, in examining your monuments as I passed by them, I found among others an altar which bore the inscription, To the unknown God. And it is this unknown object of your devotion that I am revealing to you" (Acts 17:22). Does it not seem clear, from these words, that through the history of the whole of mankind, which has one God for its creator, there runs a single pattern? So that wherever men have sought Him in sincerity and love they have discovered concerning Him some part of the truth? And applying this principle to the religions of China, the question in my mind was, Cannot Christians find in them some points of contact with Christianity; and should they not, therefore, rather adopt St. Paul's dictum than retain an attitude towards paganism that is purely negative?

My visit to the shrine of the pagan god Apollo at Delphi was another high point of my journey in Greece. This holiest spot of the ancient world dedicated to Apollo more than three thousand years ago is 152 miles from Athens, set on a sloping shelf of rock that juts out into a blue-misty gorge from two perpendicular cliffs of Mount Parnassus. Apollo was the god of health, sanity and song, athletic prowess and gallant good sense. Carved over the entrance to the temple are two famous maxims: "Know Thyself," and "Nothing Too Much." At the time these words did not capture my attention. Since I have become a Catholic, this ancient wisdom is grist to my mill.

One event touching my religious development, which perhaps interested me more than anything else at the time, was the visit to Mount Athos. About eighty miles southeast of Salonika, Mount Athos is situated on one of the three peninsulas which lie parallel to each other in the Aegean Sea. On a height overlooking the sea there are several monasteries belonging to an order of Orthodox monks. I am told that no female has been allowed on Mount Athos in centuries, not even a female animal, and the prohibition extends even to unshaven boys.

Unimportant to commerce and industry, the peninsula has been ignored by the outside world for several hundred years. The civil administrators in whose jurisdiction it falls have given it hardly a thought. From time to time in the course of this period, it has been raided by pirates, but the monasteries were so poor and the priests' life so simple, that nothing was gained by such incursions, and in the recent past even the roving guerrillas have left them strictly alone.

The priests support themselves without outside help. Agriculture is almost their only skill. The staple of their diet is corn bread, supplemented by fish and a few vegetables. When they fish, what they do not need for the day is thrown back into the sea. Only enough potatoes for one meal are dug at a time. Baking is done once a week. All is done without haste or anxiety; there is no thought of money, for the fact is that there is no currency here. It is one place in the world where money is not supreme.

But a description of the monastic life at Mount Athos would be the subject of a fascinating study all by itself. What I wish to point out here is the contrast: the Greek people on the mainland fighting in a life-and-death struggle, the docile, simple priests of Mount Athos dwelling in absolute seclusion and naïve oblivion of the outside world, and paying little attention to it. They preserve their religious traditions in complete detachment from the shocks and strain of modern industrial civilization, holding themselves in reserve even from visitors from the mainland. I remember on leaving this Utopia in the Aegean

153

the deep sense I had that the simple and religious "Mount Athosians" were enjoying something their materially rich visitors rarely obtain—peace of mind.

When the opportunity was given me, some months after my work in Greece, to make an extended tour of the Balkan countries, I set out, my first stop Sofia, with a heavy heart, convinced in advance that I should find no source of consolation in these devastated lands, from all reports full of an atmosphere of gloom. But in this I was wrong. A distinguished American friend, in constant touch with events there, told me that in spite of extremely difficult conditions, the people remained staunchly loyal to the Church. The vast majority belonged to the Orthodox Church, which had been "reorganized" since the advent of Communism and was State controlled. The small Catholic minority of about one percent of the population were, however, putting up a much more gallant fight against religious oppression. A Capuchin monastery was still carrying on, although the priests had encountered innumerable difficulties. People visited the churches more frequently than before. Homes were places of prayer more than in former times. The churches were filled not only on Sundays, but also on weekdays.

It is my deepest hope that this description of the religious life in the Balkans in 1947 would apply to the Chinese mainland today. The people are more attached to the Church than they have been for years. Suffering and oppression have driven them to seek God. In fact, it is God, in silence and Wisdom, who uses the Church's enemies to perfect His saints and purify His religion.

Perhaps the thing which impressed itself upon my memory most in Sofia was attendance at a "Gala Representation at the State Opera" given in Sofia's handsome opera house in honor of all the members of the Commission. I went with Ambassador Wunsz King and Major T. P. Wang and sat in a box twice removed from the late Prime Minister Georgi Dimitrov. The famed Bulgarian ballet we saw was based on an old native legend and, as Mrs. Ethridge put it very vividly, was performed "with so much agility and spirit it was hard to believe the performers were not dancing on live coals instead of pink lights on the stage floor."* The program closed with Bulgarian folk dances, which were remarkable for the elaborateness and beauty of the native costumes and the swiftness and vitality of the dancers' movements. As I left this scene, it was with a curious sense of heightened reality, as though all that was happening in the Balkans were like the acts of a drama, whether a comedy or tragedy remained to be seen.

---

* *It's Greek to Me* (Vanguard Press), p. 195

As the Commission had set its date to draft its Report at Geneva we had to leave Sofia by a through-train with only a few hours' stop at Belgrade. It may seem quite outside the scope of this book to describe my trip to Yugoslavia, but an episode which showed the discomforts of sitting on the fence, as it were, and acting without a principle, as the Yugoslavs did before their break with Moscow, bears recalling.

We were thirty altogether on a night train. I was fortunate enough to have my dear old friend, Harry Howard, in the compartment next to mine, so I had no need to count on my alarm clock. His typewriter never failed to make enough noise to awaken me even before dawn. No one could lodge a complaint with him. He would always justify his cause by saying: "Do you think I should not write a few lines to my Virginia and Robert?"

Not until around 2:30 p.m. the following day did we arrive in Belgrade. As there was no *wagon-lit* restaurant we had nothing to eat or drink, and everybody was most uncomfortable. We were met at the station by the Chief of Protocol of the Yugoslav Foreign Office. He guided us to a very nice-looking bus. As the train without a dining car had been arranged by the Yugoslav authorities, it was well understood by them that our stomachs were empty. We all felt happy and grateful when we learned that the bus would first take us somewhere to eat.

As we crossed town we could see that every street lamp was crowned with a red star and the walls were covered with Communist slogans. Portraits of Tito were displayed everywhere. We passed many a restaurant and hotel, but the bus kept rolling. The more it rolled, the hungrier we became. Not until we were out of the town did we become aware that we were going to Tito's summer resort, some eighty miles from the railway station, where our much-needed lunch was waiting! After a trip in which we grew faint, we arrived at the place around 4 p.m. No sooner had we got off the bus than we were ushered into the dining hall. However, we were informed that as lunch was not yet ready we might wander about for relaxation. The circumstances should have caused anxiety for the Yugoslavs, but we were so exhausted we could hardly enjoy the scenery.

After the lapse of another hour we were finally informed that the table was ready. We first gathered in the living room next to the dining hall and found nothing but cigarettes. After fifteen minutes, we were offered cocktails.

At last, the lunch was served, and the menu stands out in my memory. It included caviar, consomme, fresh tongue with wine sauce, sweetbreads rolled in butter, creamed spinach in patty shells, creamed carrots in patty shells, potatoes in small golden-brown balls, artichokes with hollandaise sauce, a bomb of cream stuffed with chestnuts and brandied candies, followed by fruits and coffee. Not one among us succeeded in plowing through to the end.

But this is not all. After the tables were cleared we were directed to reboard the bus to return to town. At about eight o'clock we reached the Majestic Hotel, where dinner was ready! We sat down and were served with caviar, fresh mushrooms on toast, fried chicken, celery stewed in clear broth and lemon juice and heavily sprinkled with parsley, potatoes, and green salad, followed by cheesecake for dessert. The waiters stared at us as we shook our heads. Dutifully, we all drank two cups of black coffee. At half-past nine we were again on the train for Trieste and Milan, en route to Geneva. Early the next morning it was not Harry's typewriter but my empty stomach that broke my dreams.

The hospitality extended to us by the Yugoslav Government could hardly be questioned, but we were really in a position neither to laugh nor to lament.

Now that I think of it, I can see that in Yugoslavia and in the Balkans as a whole there is sadness under the surface. The people find themselves on the horns of a dilemma. They are fighting on two fronts: exteriorly they are subject to the relentless pressure of atheist communism; interiorly they are in travail with the demands of religion, with that great hunger of the spirit which, through His mercy, makes itself known with the keenest pangs when Christ's Church is in danger. I cannot think of them without reciting the prayer that St. Paul wrote in his Epistle to the Ephesians, during his first imprisonment in Rome: "With this in mind, then, I fall on my knees to the Father of our Lord Jesus Christ, that Father from whom all fatherhood in heaven and on earth takes its title. May he, out of the rich treasury of his glory, strengthen you through his spirit with a prayer that reaches your innermost being. May Christ find a dwelling-place, through faith, in your hearts; may your lives be rooted in love, founded on love. May you and all the saints be enabled to measure, in all its breadth and length and height and depth, the love of Christ, to know what passes knowledge. May you be filled with all the completion God has to give. He whose power is as work in us is powerful enough, and more than powerful enough, to carry out his purpose beyond all our hopes and dreams; may he be glorified in the Church, and in Christ Jesus, to the last generation of eternity. Amen" (3:14–21). In God love, truth, and freedom are one.

When the Commission's work drew to a close in

May 1947, I was called upon to go to Lake Success to assist in the work of my delegation on the Security Council. As events were to show, this appointment was a providential one.

In New York I renewed my acquaintance with Mr. Joseph T. H. Hsieh, whom I had known in Rome when he had been there as an escort to Bishop Tien in 1946, and this association enabled me to take up again the threads of the spiritual life which Dr. Wu had done so much to encourage in me. For so long now religious considerations had been relegated to the back of my mind under the pressure of my duties in the Balkans. At least, I so excuse myself, but I wonder whether it is the real reason.

Hsieh was Vice-President of the Catholic Charities Association of Shanghai and a benefactor of China's poor. He usually spent his weekends in my home at Sea Cliff, Long Island. Each night he knelt in prayer, and sometimes he asked me to kneel too. I learned for the first time about the sign of the cross. It intrigued me, and I practised it in secret. Hsieh heard Mass with considerable frequency, and I now learned from him that what the Mass does is, by assuring the continuity of His real presence, to enable men to *live* with Christ in the Church. Nothing could be more simple, but at the same time nothing could be more profound and touching. I became aware of a very sweet, strong urging, a constant suggestion in my mind: "Why not go to Mass? Why not go to Mass?" I had lived in Europe for several years. I had been in and out of many Catholic cathedrals and churches, and yet I had never heard Mass!

I cannot easily forget the experience of a certain day. God had made it a very beautiful Sunday, and Hsieh and I proceeded to St. Patrick's Cathedral on Fifth Avenue. The sun was blazing, and the two Gothic steeples stood magnificently against a blue sky swarming with fleets of white clouds. A number of pigeons were hopping about on the Cathedral steps, and they caught my fancy. We went through the wide open door into the cool darkness, and all at once, all the churches of Italy and France and the Balkan monasteries came back to me.

It is literally true that only when one has entered the Church does he find that the Church is larger inside than it is outside. I received this impression in the physical sense as I entered St. Patrick's. Among the things that impressed me most were the stained-glass windows. They give the Cathedral the rich, festive appearance of the great cathedrals of the world. Now that I think of it, should any of these splendid windows fail to arouse appreciation, the fault surely lies not in the picture, but in the observer, who either has not grasped the historic scene, or has not understood the technique of the picture, or has missed the object of the artist.

In order not to be spotted for a pagan, I closely imitated whatever my companion, Hsieh, did. I dipped my fingers in holy water as I entered, and crossed myself, the same as Hsieh, but without true understanding. After genuflecting, we entered a pew and knelt down. For my part I was absorbed in what was going on at the altar and conscious of the attitude of the people. Hsieh was praying fervently, fully demonstrating the serious, indeed the principal, reason for going to church.

The effect on my mind was inexpressibly strange; seeing the place full, absolutely full, and all the men and women and children, young and old—especially the young—pray and pray in perfect silence. As the father of three boys I could not help wondering what force short of a miracle was there to subdue the sportive disposition of boyhood!

It seemed to me that everyone comprehended that, in the presence of the tabernacle, he ought "to be silent in order to listen to Him, and leave himself in order to lose himself in Him." In fact, everyone appeared free of constraint and more conscious of God than man. There was something more than a social gathering; the people were conscious not so much of fulfilling a human obligation as a religious one.

Although I did not understand at the time what the priest at the altar was saying and doing, what the standing-up and crossing oneself every once in a while were for, I found something in everything and everything in something. I felt that there was some kind of a Presence before me—or at least that I was in an atmosphere of great spiritual sweetness, unlike anything I had so far known.

Now and again I would overhear what the priest was saying in a solemn voice: *"Dominus Vobiscum,"* *"Oremus,"* or *"Et cum spiritu tuo."* Hsieh explained after Mass that *"Dominus Vobiscum"* is a simple greeting, "The Lord be with you." We have something like it in English in our "good-bye," which is actually a shortened form of "God be with you." *"Oremus,"* which means "Let us pray," is an invitation to take part in the prayer that is to follow. *"Et cum spiritu tuo"*—"and with your spirit"—a simple answer to the simple greetings, refers to the Church's power of blessing, which the priest has received.

I listened to all this thoughtfully, and as I pondered it the thought came to me that what I had experienced during the Mass was a sense of community: the congregation had not consisted of isolated units but had been gathered up in some way into the Sacrifice at the altar. I was able to define, in a groping way, what I had experienced, but not yet to explain it; I felt profoundly the effect of the Mass, but without under-standing. And this is typical of the whole manner of my conversion: the fact is that I began to love the Church before it occurred to me that one might love God, or even have an intelligible and rational be-lief in Him.

Now I fell into the habit of visiting Catholic churches with considerable frequency. I took delight in learning about the sacraments, liturgical forms, etc. It became something of a hobby with me to acquire in-formation about the Faith, and I read a good deal of popular apologetic literature. In the meantime, one thought was constantly reiterated in my mind: "The Church is really beautiful. The Mass is indeed signifi-cant. . . . Why not be a Catholic? . . . Why not be a Catholic?"

Human nature, however, has a way of putting for-ward clever arguments in extenuation of its unruly desires and lack of courage. It also tends to excuse our spiritual idleness, refusing to commit the cure of the sick soul to the spiritual physician, on the ground that this is not the time for action, and so our decisions are put off. Some other time. . . . Some other time. . . .

In this way my human nature was resisting the mag-net which was working in my soul: "If you keep your conscience right, really believe what the Church

teaches, this is quite enough. To believe in Catholicism
does not necessarily mean that you have to be a Catholic," I would assure myself. As I look back, I see
that never was the cart put more squarely before the
horse. As Bishop Fulton J. Sheen puts it, "To say that
we want good things but not Goodness, which is God-
ness, is like saying that we love the sunbeams but we
hate the sun, or we like the moonlight but despise the
moon." *

There is much to be said for not attempting more
than one can do and for making a certainty of what
one wishes to try. St. Augustine once said in his life,
"Dear Lord, I want to be good, but later on, not now."
I thought then that it was sufficient to conform extern-
ally to Catholic teaching and ritual. I thought I was
being virtuous and trying to preserve "purity of heart"
as far as possible. I would never become a saint;
it was enough to be good. There was another thought
I had: "Although my attachment to Catholicism is well
known to all my Catholic friends, they have never
made any attempt to persuade me to be a Catholic.
Surely the Church would be pleased to have my name
added to a parish roster. Why should I act on my own
initiative? I ought to be prudent and wait for their
invitation." In consequence, I postponed any really
energetic spiritual activity.

* *Lift Up Your Heart* (Whittlesey), p. 68.

"My entrance into the Church will bring joy to religion," and "I ought to be prudent and not enter until I am invited." How incredible my complacency and selfish calculation seem in retrospect! Under the pretext of prudence I refused to give up my life of sin, and I let myself be deceived under the pretense of doing good. I simply made myself a fugitive from faith by trying to put the responsibility elsewhere.

If I endeavor to analyze my state of mind at the time, the dual character of Stevenson's Dr. Jekyll and Mr. Hyde fits me like a glove. When a false god— ego, or self—is adored, one deliberately makes himself into a "Jekyll and Hyde" personality. As "Dr. Jekyll" he wanders around the Church door, seeking to justify his conduct by outward tokens, that his soul may be saved without a price. In his "Mr. Hyde" phase he devotes himself to nothing but self-interest. He considers the Church a citadel to serve as a refuge for self-love. Yet such was I, a son of Adam.

In this sense I used the false god to conceal my thoughts in two separate compartments. In one was the man I wanted to be. I could concentrate on the exterior without interior application, be easy and free without any sacrifice. I feared that if I put too much confidence in the Faith, the other compartment of my conscience would step in and would demand too much effort and self-discipline.

At the time I thought of myself as a free man: Had I not succeeded in making myself completely independent of any kind of religious discipline or sacrifice? If my conscience stirred, I quieted it by plunging more deeply into worldly affairs. Thus I allowed my senses excessive liberty and neglected the custody of the soul. My attitude towards religion was very much like a man knocking at the door of truth and hoping there would be no answer, or ringing God's doorbell and then running away.

As I see it now, there were two characteristic traits that were manifesting themselves in my attitude toward religion: my tendency to acquire an interest and then let it peter out; my constitutional indifference, which inclined me to push out of mind a problem that baffled me.

"So you also outwardly indeed appear to men just: but inwardly you are full of hypocrisy and iniquity" (Matt. 23:28). Was not this a faithful portraiture of the state of my soul? In this light, one can fully realize the truth of St. John's words: "But because thou art lukewarm and neither cold nor hot, I will begin to vomit thee out of my mouth" (Apoc. 3:16). My lukewarmness persisted, and I clung to my condition.

Nobody has more clearly described the order of salvation among Christians than St. Paul, who says: "Not that we are sufficient to think of anything of ourselves, as of ourselves" (2 Cor. 3:15) and "It is God who worketh in you, both to will and to accomplish" (Phil. 2:13). I continued to be preoccupied with myself, and where the pursuits of a man aim for ego-centered seeing, he does not achieve enlightened seeing. Unless a man's heart becomes disengaged from the flesh, it cannot freely attend to the spirit. If there are any laws of the spiritual universe, certainly this is one of them.

XII

Bombs in the Balkans

*"Fear ye not them that kill
the body and are not able to
kill the soul: but rather fear
him that can destroy both soul
and body in hell"* (Matt.
10:28).

The process of maturing in the religious sense is more
than the process of receiving impressions, one after
another. It involves the savoring of these impressions
until their meaning and bearing are realized; letting
new experiences turn around and around in the restless heart and soul until the meaningful facet shows itself. And when maturity comes, all the elements of
our experience leap into focus and we see it in its
integrity; then we become convinced of the truth of
St. Augustine's dictum that God has made us for Himself, and our hearts are restless till they rest in Him.
I shall now go on to describe how I trod a zigzag
course on my spiritual journey, and how God, in His
prevenient grace, bestowed upon me every opportunity
in small, day-by-day events to respond to His solicita-
tions.

In September 1947 I finished the business with my delegation on the U. N. Security Council and was recalled to China by my government to report on my duties. Before I left New York, I was invited to broadcast to China over the U. N. radio station about conditions in the Balkans. I cannot remember my exact words on that occasion, but the substance of my talk was this: "Materialism is endeavoring to win over the world through its social program, and we who claim to fight in the cause of free, democratic institutions have failed to draw strength from the realm of ideas. We, even more than the materialists, think and work in material terms. The free world must be rebuilt from its foundations." An astonishingly wise and virtuous observation from someone as unvirtuous as myself: but it is remarkable how easy it is to be idealistic when one's idealism is an externalized thing, making no demands on one's own mind and will. But at any rate, I am today even more firmly convinced of the truth of my analysis.

On my trip to China, God ordained that I should travel by air in Hsieh's company. We stopped at various places, including San Francisco, Honolulu, Midway, Wake, Guam, and so on. The first thing Hsieh did at each stop was to find a church and hear Mass, if there were a Mass. Strangely enough, there most often was. I must confess that, cherishing the Jekyll-

Hyde type of living, I went along more as a matter of courtesy toward Hsieh than an act of faith toward God. However, I was much impressed to discover that the Mass offered in St. Patrick's in New York and the one on a little island in the Pacific could be easily recognized as identical, even by an outsider like myself. Since becoming a Catholic, I have realized that this is a consequence of the Church's constant, purposeful conservation of doctrine, her careful guardianship of the whole treasure of revelation. But even then I thought the achievement most extraordinary.

In Shanghai, I had the good fortune of meeting Mr. Soong Han-chang, General Manager of the Bank of China. He is a convert of Lo Pa-hung's, and entered the Church some thirty years ago. Today at seventy-eight, he still visits the sick and suffering daily. I worked at the Bank of China from 1931 to 1934, while I spent my evenings studying law in the Comparative Law School of China in Shanghai, so Soong was really my old boss. This time, I called on him as representing not so much a former employer as a pious Catholic. I admired him not only for his virtue of charity, but for his devotion to God's cause in general.

Soong kindly invited me to lunch and had me speak on International Relations and World Peace to a gathering of some three hundred of the bank staff. As this speech represents my philosophy of life in relation to world politics, I want to reproduce a part of it here.

"All governments today pay equal lip-service to the common purpose of promoting international peace. Every one of them, if challenged, can point to laws and policies that are noble beyond criticism. Each side assumes that the other side should understand its peaceful intentions, though it is clearly evident that each is still as suspicious of the other as ever. In reality all of them are hindering each other. As confidence decreases, there is a race for armament—atomic weapons, which leaves the souls of all fearful and uncertain.

"How can we account for this? Evidently the things which cause anguish in nations or cause nations to engage in conflicts with each other have their origin in the sins of individuals.

"In Chinese there are two sides to the coin of peace, one is harmony, and the other is equality; if one is defective, the coin is spurious. The principle by which like entities are attracted to each other and opposites respect each other is 'harmony.' 'Equality' obtains if the strong do not bully the weak and the many do not oppress the few. This typically Chinese conception of 'harmony and equality' enables mankind, through purely moral channels, to live and let live, and to make common progress among themselves.

"Many there are today who would try to impose their idea of peace on others, by physical or material means. But we must know that physical means cannot make people equal, nor can material gains make them harmonious. What is worse, if any country should impose its own particular brand of ideology upon another, or if it threatens to bully the weak or persecute the minority by the employment of deliberate methods, that is in direct contravention to the true spirit of peace. Peace can never be attained in that way.

"What do we find in the world today? We find that human love—parental, brotherly, and marital—is daily on the decline. Here and there, we hear preached the strange doctrine that Christian morality should be repudiated and a new ethics to suit the unethical or chaotic lives of a very few individuals should be developed. Once love, both human and Divine, flies from a man, it is impossible for him to love nobly or live a noble life. That being so, how could we then expect to maintain a healthy personal and family and community life? If close blood-relationship is unable to serve as a cementing force, no wonder that the distance between men and men, or between community

175

and community, tends to widen. When people go to such lengths and without scruple, how can world peace avoid becoming hopeless?

"So if we wish to create a permanent peace and to avert another world castastrophe, we must proceed from the bottom up by the restoration of sound family life, which can be achieved only by a recovery on the part of individual human beings of a personal consciousness of unity, of the fundamental truth—'Thou shalt love thy neighbor as thyself.' For peace is the fruit of charity. The hatred that has been engendered and fostered in so many hearts is not going to be overcome by additional and stronger hatred. It is not going to be checked and destroyed by material might, but only by patience, understanding, confidence, generosity, self-sacrifice, and by bringing love back to its rightful place in man's relationship to man. Only when man realizes that he is composed of body and soul, that his real and lasting achievements are in the realm of the spirit; when the world places the character of man above the value of his products, measures material accomplishments by their effect on man himself, recognizes the necessity of mutual love, both human and Divine, can men enjoy the fruits of physical prosperity on earth and be able to defend themselves against any kind of terrifying weapon. Otherwise material progress may become the

176

enemy of human life itself, and the victory of technology may mean the destruction of humanity, since it is impossible to ignore the way in which the latest triumphs of applied science have been turned to destructive ends. The recognition of our deeply-felt interior poverty in spite of exterior riches is the beginning of hope.

"The times in which we live must be painted in the somber values of Rembrandt. The background is dark, the shadows deep, outlines are obscure. The central point, however, glows with light; and, though it often brings out the glint of steel, it touches colors of unimaginable beauty. For us, that central point is the growing unity of men in the love of God. This is our shaft of light, our hope and our promise."

As I look back now, I am astonished to realize that I delivered the speech as a full-fledged Christian. In fact, the Holy Spirit was speaking through my lips.

The winter of 1947–1948 marked an important milestone in my religious journey. It began with my appointment as the Head of the Chinese Delegation to the United Nations Special Committee on the Balkans. Here a new sphere opened to me. Here I was fed with innumerable cups of the "milk of consolation." It is not possible to pursue the Balkan story in detail. Suffice it to say here that the establishment of the Special

Committee was on the basis of the Report of the first U. N. Commission of Investigation on Greece.

I used to think of the United Nations' dealing with the case of Greece in this way: the U. N. was a medical clinic, the Greek situation the patient. The first Commission of Investigation was the physician sent to diagnose the case. Result: the Special Committee acted as nurse appointed to administer the medicine as prescribed. The Committee consisted of representatives of Australia, Brazil, China, France, Mexico, the Netherlands, Pakistan, the United Kingdom and the United States. Seats were held open for Poland and Soviet Russia. Poland and Soviet Russia declared they would not take part in the Committee's work. The nurse, therefore, was herself a cripple. Principal headquarters for the Committee were established at Salonika on December 1, 1947. I arrived there from China some twenty days later.

The Committee was given a twofold task: (1) the conciliatory role of assisting the four governments of Albania, Bulgaria, Greece, and Yugoslavia to implement the recommendations of the General Assembly—namely, to establish normal diplomatic and good-neighborly relations, to establish frontier conventions for the peaceful settlement of the problems arising out of the presence of refugees in the four states concerned, through voluntary repatriation, and to study the practicability of voluntary transfer of minorities; (2) the observation of compliance with the recommendations by the four governments concerned.

This second role, observation, caused the Committee to decide upon the establishment of observation groups near and on both sides of the frontier of the four governments, in order to observe to what extent good-neighborly relations existed on these frontiers. They were the ears and eyes of the Committee.

Efforts to obtain cooperation from Albania, Bulgaria, and Yugoslavia in the conciliatory work of the Committee had so far been unavailing. The three northern governments had also refused permission for the observation groups to operate on their territory. The groups were thus obliged to work along the Greek side of the frontier only. This meant that the patient's door was closed; the nurse had to wait outside. No one knew where the key to the door was.

From the beginning of its work in Greece the Committee was confronted by the political implications of the formation, announced on December 24, 1947, of a so-called "Provisional Democratic Greek Government," headed by the then Greek Communist leader, Markos. In order that the Committee should not be caught unaware by a *fait accompli* of recognition of the Markos government by the northern neighbors of

179

Greece, a resolution was adopted to the effect that any such recognition might lead the Committee to recommend the convocation of a special session of the General Assembly as a matter of urgency, a power granted the Committee in its terms of reference.

The Greeks had no delusions about the source of the so-called "civil war," by which the countries to the north tried to maintain the disorganization of Greek life. So the Committee's resolution, which stood guard on their territorial integrity and political independence, must have met with their approval, with the exception of one man, Markos. His disapproval was manifested by a sudden assault on the Committee's headquarters in Salonika in the February of the following year. How narrow our escape was in reality can be gathered from some of the facts we came to know only afterwards.

My diary notes that about two o'clock in the morning, I was awakened by a vivid flash of lightning. My rooms rang with the reports of firearms and the crash of breaking windows. Before I could get up, a shell exploded so near that it almost threw me out of bed. I sat up. Sleep fled my eyes as I began to take in what was happening. I hustled into my clothes and rushed out to the Conference room where all my colleagues were gathering. The dark paneling of the room, illuminated only by a few lamps, threw into sharp relief the chaotic scene of that night. It is strange, the things one remembers from a time of emergency. I have a vivid recollection of Sir Horace Seymour, Chief Delegate to the British Delegation and former Ambassador to China, wearing a Chinese gown, in sandals without socks, puffing incessantly at his unlighted Macedonian cigarette. Psychologically, the event caught us all flat-footed.

Flares ignited by the blast were falling in the streets and lay burning on the buildings around the port, their greens and scarlets reflected by the glistening surface of the sea. Flames began to leap up, and tiny stars of incredible intensity, showered out of the inferno, were shimmering and dancing all through the city. The sky became like a huge sheet of sickly amber flame.

After about an hour the guns were silent, and quiet settled over the place. There is no getting to the bottom of most things that happen in Greece. Just how the near outskirts of Salonika got into the hands of a band of roving guerrillas, how they could possibly have attacked the U. N. Committee's headquarters at such close range, will never be known. All we learned was that a band of some six hundred guerrillas, camped about two miles from the city wall, had had the Committee's headquarters—the Mediterranean Palace—as their target. About fifteen mortar shells dropped within a radius of fifty metres of the Palace. One exploded on the grounds right in front of my bedroom. We had had a bad scare, but nobody was hurt.

This incident is not presented here as a matter of theological study; I do not maintain that it is evidence of direct divine intervention in my life. But for me it had been of great significance that, had the shell been aimed a trifle higher, it would have been a direct hit on my room. Where should I have been then?

My narrow escape recalled to my mind the experience in the Salonika plane, which had first brought me to the realization of the need for prayer, and now grace was given to me without my praying for it. Superhuman help enlightened me interiorly, that I might see more clearly the truth that the infinite grandeur of God lies precisely in His transforming influence upon man's life. I felt an inner certainty that through prayer one drew upon supernatural power from a realm inaccessible to our human nature unaided. From this time on, I began to depend increasingly on God, although I was still far from leading a religious life. This may be the place to describe how prayer has helped me in my public life, how many favors I asked, and how much of the "milk of consolation" I received at this stage.

I have already said that altogether there were nine

countries represented on the Committee, with two seats kept open for Soviet Russia and Poland. Committee opinion on many issues was equally divided, and this frequently placed me in the position of casting the decisive vote. One morning in February 1948, a public meeting was scheduled to debate the interpretation of the Committee's mandate. Some officials predicted that the debate would end in a split and expose to the world at large the ineffectiveness of the United Nations as an organ for promoting international cooperation and world peace. This was no joke.

The point at issue was this: four delegations contended that (1) the Committee should concern itself only with observing to what extent good-neighborly relations existed between these four countries; (2) the observation groups' activities should be confined only to observation and should not include investigation; (3) as the observation groups were not judicial courts, no legal term such as "evidence" or "witness" should appear in the groups' reports. The opposite opinion on each of these points had the support of the other four delegations. They argued that the Committee was competent not only to observe good-neighborly relations between the four governments but also to investigate any alleged border incidents along the northern frontier of Greece; and that, therefore, the observation groups should be free to investigate and to hear any kind of witness for the fulfillment of their duties. The two parties held strictly to their respective grounds. There seemed to be no solution in the given circumstances.

I realized the difficulty which faced us, and early that morning I prayed earnestly for strength, and to discover a method of compromise to save the situation. After praying, I went to an office where four delegations were discussing their common front of debate. I urged them to give me the chance to submit a plan before the debate was opened. Then I visited the other group of four delegations, who were also preparing for the debate. I made the same appeal, and they promised to consider the plan.

When the meeting opened under the Chairmanship of Sir Horace Seymour, I moved an amendment to the agenda to the effect that the general debate on the mandate should be avoided. This was accepted. Then I made a strong appeal for conciliation and introduced a compromise measure.

Among other things, I said: "The wax as well as the flame is necessary if a candle is to burn. The flame of the Committee is still burning, but the wax has got rather low lately, and I fear that if it gets too low the flame may go out. The extraordinary conciliatory spirit shown by my colleagues in agreeing to my first proposal regarding the agenda has increased the flame and the wax, and thus inspired me to put forward proposals which, I hope, will help towards a compromise.

"The Committee, I know, is conscious of the supreme task entrusted to it by the United Nations, and the fact that the latter's fate is closely tied to the success of the Committee. It is, therefore, not surprising that an honest exchange of views has taken place in order, on the one hand, to avoid criticism on the grounds of lack of impartiality and, on the other, to make every effort to discharge the responsibility given to the Committee by the General Assembly. Differences of opinion must always be admitted in the discussion of any issue, but the question before the Committee is how, in this case, it can fulfill its task to the fullest extent without going beyond its terms of reference and its legal implications.

"My proposals are guided by two purposes; first, that the work of the observation group, which I have followed with sympathy and appreciation, should not be jeopardized; and secondly, that the Committee should not act inconsistently with its original intention."

Following this statement I detailed my proposal as follows: "Firstly, besides being entrusted to observe to what extent good-neighborly relations exist, the observation groups are also competent to observe any

185

alleged incident, or suspected incidents involving *a breach of* those relations.

"Secondly, as there is only a difference of degree between 'observation' and 'investigation'—an exhaustive observation may be equal to an investigation, and a less intensive investigation may be just the same as an observation—the groups' activities shall be hereafter described as 'observation' instead of 'investigation,' in order to follow the nomenclature given to them.

"Thirdly, the word 'information' should be substituted for words such as 'evidence' and 'witness,' for, since the groups are not judicial bodies, it is advisable to avoid using legal terms in their mandate. However, gathering information covers a wide field and will not exclude interviews with the public or questioning and receiving replies from those concerned."

My proposals, such as they were, seemed quite satisfactory to one party because, according to these proposals, the Committee should not concern itself with border incidents. Furthermore, all the terms regarding investigation had been replaced by the word "observation." On the other hand, they seemed acceptable also to the other party, for they did not differ much from their original view in respect of the competence of the observation groups. For example, my proposals implied that the Committee might only observe good-neighborly relations and might not investigate any border incident, but it might observe any alleged incidents involving *a breach of* good-neighborly relations. Of course there was practically no difference between a border incident and an incident involving *a breach of* good-neighborly relations. So far as the competence of the observation groups was concerned, my proposals implied also that while they might not hear witnesses or testimony, they were entitled to gather information, which might entail interviews with the public, or questioning and receiving replies from those concerned. In other words, I had simply issued a fresh prescription, containing the same drugs as the old one, but in liquid form!

To the satisfaction of all my colleagues, the compromise was unanimously approved. Both parties thus came to terms. After that the Committee worked smoothly.

As I see it now, it is hardly credible that my personal intervention should have exercised such great influence on my colleagues. It is unreasonable to suppose that these effects were achieved by any means but prayer. It seems simple, but it is adequate, for this is the method of Christ.

One recollection leads to another, all of which at the time had seemed isolated instances. In April 1949, a new delegate was scheduled to preside over a public

meeting in Salonika. The man, an outstanding diplomat with ambassadorial rank, had joined the Committee to challenge its general policy. His public
attack, if not well defended, would place the Committee in an awkward position and its future in jeop-
ardy. Many of the delegates feared the outcome of
this meeting.

About an hour before the meeting, I prayed. My
prayer was a mixture of anticipating God's help with
hope and desire and imagining how the situation
would shape up. In fact, it was the type of prayer
best suited to myself. Then I typed three pages of the
thoughts that occurred to me during my prayers.

When the meeting opened, the outspoken Chairman
took full advantage of his position. He spoke unre-
servedly against the general opinion. The Committee
had established two Sub-Committees and one Advisory
Committee. Each of these was composed of five delegations. Only China sat on all three. As the Chief
Chinese delegate, I was the Chairman of the Advisory
Committee, which dealt with some of the most important controversial questions. Therefore, the charges
were focused more or less on my position.

As soon as he had finished, I took the floor. Without
any change, I read my written statement. It answered,
point by point, the Chairman's charges.

After my speech, one of the delegates asked for

the floor. While endorsing my argument, he complained of the discrimination shown in allowing any delegate prior access to the Chairman's speech. He thought that I had obtained a copy in advance to prepare a written reply. The Chairman immediately protested that he had not prepared any written speech beforehand. He said he had formulated his ideas only half an hour before the meeting.

This is additional testimony to the power of divine grace, and through it I experienced joy very hard to describe.* These are but two among many instances of the divine assistance God has generously bestowed upon me when I have called upon Him through prayer. And I can testify that once the heart is wholly devoted to prayer, results will be achieved far beyond anything one can plan or imagine. But it must not be supposed that my efforts in prayer have been uniformly successful; when self-love intrudes itself and the intention of prayer loses its purity, the consequences are bitter and humiliating, and the prayer itself becomes scarcely more than a form of daydreaming. Here is an example of my failure:

This incident took place not long before the assassi-

---

* St. Thomas says: "Whoever receives it (grace) knows, by experiencing a certain sweetness, which is not experienced by one who does not receive it." (See *Summa Theologica* Ia, IIae, q. 112, a. 5.)

nation in Jerusalem on September 17, 1948, of Count Folke Bernadotte, who had been acting as the United Nations mediator. As representative of China, I had submitted to the Committee a draft resolution to the effect that the Committee should give its full support to Secretary-General Mr. Trygve Lie's proposal to the General Assembly for the creation of a permanent United Nations Guard in order to insure the efficient operation of an adequate protection for field missions. Two outstanding considerations were in my mind when I drafted the proposal—first, experience had shown that a more systematic and stronger service must be provided for the field missions by the Secretariat; secondly, once the United Nations had its own field force, a heavy burden would have been lifted from the shoulders of the big powers, especially the United States, which had contributed disproportionately to the ranks of mission members.

I first discussed at length the draft outline in advance with the other eight delegations. In a spirit of harmony and mildness, they generously gave their approval in general to my proposal. Before the meeting was held I prayed for a unanimous adoption of my proposal, but I confess that in my prayer I was engaged more in contemplating the political glory which would come to me through its adoption than the benefits which would be derived by the nations.

I was seeking my own advancement rather than trying to discover how the international interest should best be served. So it was not a prayer at all. Without morality there can be no true mysticism; where there is no personal virtue there is no prayer.

Notwithstanding the fact that when my proposal was put to discussion it was immediately seconded by the United States Delegation, which was ably represented by my dear friend Mr. Gerald A. Drew,* some of the other delegations, including Pakistan and the United Kingdom, in view of the complexity and importance of the questions raised by my proposal, suggested that the matter be deferred to a subsequent meeting, as they would like further time in which to give it their full consideration. Now actually there was no time element involved in my proposal, and I should have had no difficulty at all in agreeing to the deferment suggested by my colleagues. Furthermore, in order that a unanimous vote should be obtained, which would give the proposal greater weight when accepted, it was only natural that my colleagues should be allowed time for a full study. However, I did not think in this way. I was preoccupied with the next morning's headlines, with the personal success elaborated in my prayer, and therefore I took the

---

* The U.S. delegation was first headed by my distinguished friend Admiral Alan G. Kirk.

proposed deferment of the discussion as tantamount to a challenge and insisted that the matter be disposed of at the present meeting.

My intransigence left the Committee no choice but to adopt, by five votes for, two against, and two abstentions, a resolution proposed by the British Delegation. The resolution thus adopted simply watered down my original proposal and made it nearly senseless. Among the five affirmative votes for the adoption of the British resolution was the United States, which had previously endorsed my original proposal. I had driven my comrade into the opposite party. Obviously I had lost my battle. The humiliation I had caused myself made it impossible for me to remain inwardly unruffled, even though my colleagues were not provoked with me.

On a point of order, I contended that I could not accept the British proposal as an amendment, since it was against the whole spirit of my draft resolution. I would, therefore, regard it as an independent resolution of the British representative, and I accordingly asked the Committee to vote again on my resolution. To this, the Principal Secretary, Mr. Raoul Aglion, replied, affirming that I had correctly interpreted the Rules of Procedure.

This, of course, put most of my colleagues in a rather embarrassing position, for in one way or another they had given their general oral approval to my draft outline in our private consultations before the meeting. The United States Delegation, which had first endorsed my original proposal and then voted for the British resolution, would find special difficulty facing the issue. In view of the difficult situation, the British delegate said that he had pressed for deferment in the first place because he felt that the proposal was a far-reaching one which needed further consideration. He asked now that the meeting be adjourned.

If I had treated my colleagues with due regard, as they had treated me, I should have agreed with the British delegate, who was so considerate as to suggest adjournment as a way of solution. But I was stuck fast in the mire of my egoism and in no mood to cherish the rights of others. I was unwilling to yield any ground for a compromise, even if it would be to the advantage of my proposal, nor was I interested in the question of what course could best be taken by the Committee, but only in vindicating my self-importance and re-affirming my own opinions. The more I concentrated on myself, the more irritated I became with my colleagues. Like a perfect egoist, I forced the issue without looking ahead at the consequences of my action. In some show of exasperation I stated: "If the United Kingdom representative would *withdraw his resolution* which has just been adopted,

I would consent to defer my request for a vote on my own original resolution until a subsequent meeting."

Now to ask my colleagues to withdraw their proposal and the Committee as a whole to cancel its vote and re-open the discussion, a measure which called for a two-thirds majority vote, was not an ordinary matter. Only because I was so full of illusions and pride did I dare to make such a bold-faced statement so abruptly and impose such unbearable burdens upon the others. I wonder now whether I was myself that day. However, the extraordinary tolerance and mildness of my colleagues, especially my dear British colleague, who bore the affront meekly, made the Committee concede the point in my favor.

In the Committee's minutes it was thus recorded: "The United Kingdom representative agreed to withdraw the proposal which had been adopted and a vote to re-open the discussion at a subsequent meeting was carried by eight in favor with one abstention."

After the meeting many friends congratulated me on my parliamentary success in completely reversing the Committee's decision within such a short time as was seldom seen in the history of any international body. For my part, I knew only too well that I was behaving like a peacock, with an ugly voice, but strutting in his vanity. But what was done was done.

Did this self-idolatry which disguised itself under

the pretty name of "success through a technicality" make me happy? I cannot say that I was miserable. But my elation was short-lived. Although I had succeeded in gaining temporal applause and living in the eyes and in the mouths of men, my interior harmony was shattered. I felt only shamed before my colleagues, who had behaved so sweetly as to turn the left cheek to me when I struck them on the right. I had learned the salutary lesson that one who is not humble will end by being abject. I cannot think of this incident without recalling the expressive words of Father Tanquerey: "When the sentiments of pride develop, God frequently takes it upon Himself to bring back such souls to a right sense of their unworthiness and their insufficiency, by depriving them of consolation and of choice graces. Then they realize that they are as yet far removed from the desired goal." *

Perhaps one of the most accurate descriptions of my spiritual state in those years is found in T. E. Brown's lines:

"If thou couldst empty all thyself of self,
  Like to a shell dishabited
  Then might He find thee on the ocean shelf
  And say: 'This is not dead,'

---

* *The Spiritual Life,* by Father Adolphe Tanquerey (Newman), p. 467.

And fill thee with Himself instead.
But thou art all replete with very thou
And hast such shrewd activity
That when He comes He says: 'This is enow
Unto itself: Twere better let it be
It is so small and full, there is no room for Me.' "

Truly, before I became less sure of myself, or at least more pliant to His will, I had need of much greater trials, more generously accepted. After my initial experiments in prayer I had a long way to travel before I should receive greater graces.

XIII

Crash and Crisis

"I say to thee, unless a man be born again of water and the Holy Ghost, he cannot enter into the kingdom of God" (*John 3:5*).

The foregoing account of my noble belief and ignoble backslidings, of my inspiring faith and my failure to live up to that faith, of my spiritual triumph and unspiritual self-defeats simply shows how incapable I was of grasping the *fullness* of the truth that had been offered to me. For lack of a congenial religious milieu I drifted away from my first love. In a multitude of ways, I did what I ought not to have done and left undone what I ought to have done—thereby compounding friction rather than harmony, falsehood rather than truth, and losing myself completely in the labyrinths of life. For example, I was completely aware that God is the Author of all good, but I could not realize that this knowledge would produce nothing but self-centered speculation, arid and sterile, if it led to no efficacious love of Him or solicitude in serving Him. I desired to be lifted from the living hell that I had made for myself, but I did not want the discipline of Catholicism. I desired to be saved, but not at the price of a cross—Christ without the nails. I prayed only for favors; I sought Him only in need. I was like a hunting dog eager in running down the hare, but devouring it instead of returning with it to his master; a sick man refusing the operation which will restore his health because he dreads the pain that is the price of health.

But the truth of the matter is that there are no short cuts to spirituality; pain and purification go hand in hand. Only when pain strikes the inner recesses of the human heart will man begin to tear off the mask of hypocrisy, become aware of sin and his own guilt, and seek for a cure. So God must intervene for man's salvation. As Bishop Fulton J. Sheen puts it, "When a soul in sin, under the impetus of grace, turns to God, there is penance; but when a soul in sin refuses to change, God sends chastisement." *

In my case—a helpless Jekyll-Hyde who was simply playing with his soul—a warning, or "a crisis," as St. Augustine calls it, if not a chastisement, was absolutely necessary, in order to let in upon me the whole brilliance of the true light. Here is His treatment.

---

* *Peace of Soul* (McGraw-Hill), p. 245.

One day in 1949 my merry new Chrysler—latest model, four-door sedan, with white sidewall tires— was delivered to me in Rome. In Europe those days a new American automobile was quite a luxury. I felt so proud of myself in my prosperity! I took my wife and our three sons—two of them had come from their school in London—and we set out for Northern Italy on a vacation. Secretly, I was as exultant over the opportunity of exhibiting the new car as I was over the prospect of the enjoyment we should have on the trip.

I had an Italian chauffeur of considerable experience, and from Rome to Milan we had a pleasant drive. But as we left Milan for Stresa, via Lake Como, I saw that the *Autostrada* was wide, smooth and straight, and the irresistible temptation came upon me to drive myself. I had taken some driving lessons at Lake Success and had been fortunate enough to secure a license from the Motor Vehicle Bureau of Mineola, New York in 1947, but not since then had I had any further practice. My chauffeur was a cautious fellow. When I expressed my willingness to drive, he showed some reluctance. However, as soon as I told him that I had a New York driving license he surrendered completely. My wife knew only too well the real value of my license, but she did not want to discourage me. She therefore advised me to drive only on the *Auto-*

strada from Milan to the outskirts of Como. It was so agreed; I hopped into the driver's seat and took the wheel. I threw in the clutch, shifted back and forth in neutral to key myself, then into low, giving it gas, as I gradually released the clutch. We were on our way along the *Autostrada* and toward Como.

The road was clear with no traffic at all. Though I seldom smoked, I now lit up a cigarette to show what a poised and experienced driver I was. All went well until we reached the outskirts of Como. I should then have turned the wheel over to the chauffeur, who sat beside me. But the driving had been too easy, I hadn't had enough occasion to exhibit my capability in the eyes of others, so I insisted on driving into town. It was usual for me to play a dominant role in the family, so my wife was not in a position to raise any objection. She had to submit her reluctance to my pleasure. However, she told me later on how frightened she had been and how she had awaited my decision with her heart in her mouth. (How many secret tears she must have shed for my inexcusable vices!)

As I drove toward town we came to a short slope. I was so preoccupied with myself that I was scarcely aware of my own movements in space; my great hope was that I should meet no obstacles, since I had not the slightest idea of what to do if I did. The great problem was that as we flew down the slope I felt quite unsure whether to make a right or a left turn. Before I could seek advice from my chauffeur, I saw ahead, at the end of the slope, a pile of water-work pipes. In fact, they seemed to be rushing to meet me. No turn either right or left was now possible.

"Slow down! Can't you see you are coming to the end? Put on your brake . . . your *brake!*" my chauffeur warned.

I shot my foot forward at once, but unfortunately instead of applying it to the brake, I put it on the gas. With lightning swiftness the car leaped forward, broke the side-traffic mark, jumped the water-work pipes, then landed on a height, at a dead stop; then I applied the emergency brake as a matter of course.

The screams from the back seat were deafening. With the abrupt stop, all the occupants of the car except myself—since I had the advantage of holding the steering wheel—had bounced up and whacked their heads on the roof of the car. They would have been thrown straight through had there been an opening. Their cries were presently supplemented from outside. A crowd was pushing in to view the spectacle.

It seemed a miracle that anyone could have been unhurt. Almost equally miraculous was the fact that the car escaped injury; it was unscathed as if nothing had happened. Could any obstacle in the world other than the water-work pipes have served the purpose of slowing down the car so adequately that the motor stopped automatically, without the application of the emergency brake? Had there been a tree, a house—in fact anything but the pipes—could catastrophe have been avoided?

The incident taught me a profound lesson in humility. It tore off the Jekyll-Hyde mask. To have a lesson brings distress, but to experience it brings hope. The roots of experience are bitter, but its fruits sweet. As soon as we returned to Milan I went alone to the Duomo Cathedral in the center of the city. How can I describe the peace of this citadel of goodness? In crossing the threshhold I entered a realm of brooding and mysterious tranquillity. On my knees before the altar I tried to adjust my confused thoughts to the horrible event which had just occurred and left me so shaken. Candles flickered before the statues of the saints in their niches; the brass doors of the tabernacle gleamed in the soft radiance of the sanctuary lamp; white flowers spread their subtle fragrance. Nothing could have been more healing to my bruised senses than the atmosphere of this house; nothing could have been more clarifying to my inward vision than the peace and silence it enclosed.

Conflicting feelings were surging in me. Gratitude for the narrow escape; sorrow for my repeated acts offensive to the love of God. I lamented as bitterly as Lord Ullin in the poem,* but for different reasons, and I spoke to myself in reproach and sorrow. Had anyone observed me, he might have thought I had been suffering long-enduring pain.

The thought uppermost in my mind was that by rights, everybody should have been killed in our head-on collision. I felt like a criminal. I thought that so long as I kept the car, I should live in constant expectation of being held for murder.

As I thought how generous the love of the Savior had been in preserving me and the others from the consequences of my self-will, I felt myself strongly led to return Him love for love. "How often has He forgiven you?" I asked myself bitterly; "helped you in temptation, protected you from evil surroundings and given you opportunities for your welfare, spiritual and temporal—all this shows how loving and gracious God has been to you. And how foolish, indifferent, and ungrateful you are to abuse such mercy and goodness, purchased by the blood of Christ for you. You are really the author of the crucifixion. You have sinned exceedingly in thought, word and deed, through your fault, through your fault, through your grievous fault."

---

* Thomas Cambell's "Lord Ullin's Daughter."

Time slipped away and the agitation of my penitence, even, slipped away with it. Now it is easy enough to relate what we say in our minds when we have come into the presence of the Blessed Sacrament full of concern, with so much to say. But when we have said it all and become quiet, and are suddenly conscious that we are not quite alone—that there is here Someone closer to us than we are to ourselves: it is not possible to find words to describe an encounter so interior. We can only say, with the Psalmist:

"The Lord is nigh unto them that are of a contrite
heart: and he will save the humble of spirit"
(Ps. 33:19).

". . . the Lord hath heard the voice of my weeping.
The Lord hath heard my supplication: the Lord hath
received my prayer" (Ps. 6: 9–10).

But as I knelt there it came to me, as a matter of quiet conviction, that I was changed. "And I said, Now have I begun: this change is of the right hand of the Most High" (Ps. 76:11).

As I slowly emerged from the church into the last rays of sunset, I was full of a sense of fresh union with God. It is not easy to express the manner in which one experiences the conviction of the truths of faith. Perhaps St. Bernard's description gives some insight into a process which the ordinary convert is powerless to describe: "Not in any figure, but infused into the soul: the Word is apprehended not under any outward appearance but by His effect—He is a Word that does not sound in the ear but penetrates the mind; He does not speak, He acts; He does not make Himself heard in the senses but in the desires of the will. His face has not a visible form but impresses a form upon the soul; it does not strike the eyes of the body but fills the heart with joy." *

That same night I felt restless, my mind and imagination so overactive that I could not go to sleep. In the quiet of the night I came to an overwhelming sense of how much time I had wasted on trivial things —how my energies had been dissipated—how my mind could have been illumined if it had not spent itself in the chitchat of the cocktail hour, if I had not been caught up in the Jekyll-Hyde existence I had been living. In this discovery I was aided by a chance reading. I opened the New Testament at random, and came upon a passage most suitable for my state:

The knowledge of God is clear to their minds; God himself has made it clear to them; from the foundations of the world men have caught sight of his invisible nature, his eternal power and his divineness, as they are known through his creatures. Thus there is no excuse for them; although they had the knowl-

---

* In Cant., XXXI, No. 6.

edge of God, they did not honor him or give thanks
to him as God; they became fantastic in their notions,
and their senseless hearts grew benighted; they, who
claimed to be so wise, turned fools, and exchanged
the glory of the imperishable God for representations
of perishable man, of bird and beast and reptile. That
is why God abandoned their lustful hearts to filthy
practices of dishonouring their own bodies among
themselves. They had exchanged God's truth for a lie,
reverencing and worshipping the creature in prefer-
ence to the Creator (blessed is he for ever, Amen);
and, in return, God abandoned them to passions which
brought dishonor to themselves (Rom. 1:19–26).

I turned some pages and read on:

A man cannot be the slave of two masters at once;
either he will hate the one and love the other, or he
will devote himself to the one and despise the other.
You must serve God or money; you cannot serve both.
I say to you, then, do not fret over your life, how to
support it with food and drink, over your body, how
to keep it clothed. Is not life itself a greater gift than
food, the body than clothing? See how the birds of
the air never sow, or reap, or gather grain into barns,
and yet your heavenly Father feeds them; have you
not an excellence beyond theirs? Can any one of you,
for all his anxiety, add a cubit's growth to his height?
And why should you be anxious over clothing? See
how the lilies of the field grow; they do not toil or
spin; and yet I tell you that even Solomon in all his
glory was not arrayed like one of these. If God, then,

so clothes the grasses of the field, which to-day live and will feed the oven to-morrow, will he not be much more ready to clothe you, men of little faith? Do not fret, then, asking, What are we to eat? or What are we to drink? or How shall we find clothing? It is for the heathen to busy themselves over such things; you have a Father in heaven who knows that you need them all. Make it your first care to find the kingdom of God, and his approval, and all these things shall be yours without the asking. Do not fret, then, over to-morrow; leave to-morrow to fret over its own needs; for to-day, to-day's troubles are enough (Matt 6:24–34).

The vocabulary seemed new. The explanations of human misbehavior were, in many respects, new to me. Yet the pattern of life expressed was surprisingly familiar; it sounded like an old refrain to my interior ear; I had heard it all before. It had taught me, in the main, three things: to put my trust in God; not to become worked up over worries concerning the future; to know—and this is the foundation for the other two—that God is a good Father. To all these ideas, as a matter of fact, I gave voice daily, or on great occasions delivered them as axioms of wisdom. "Why, then, with these inspired truths long since known," I asked myself, "should I continue to create misery for myself and others by failing to put them into action?" The question was not a new one, but tonight it seemed quite unanswerable—that is, it was answerable in only one way. I had a clear sense that I had now reached the point of returning to God.

Looking backward in a mood of introspection and self-analysis, I recalled the forced landing of the plane, the mortar shelling of the guerrillas, the reading of *The Science of Love*, the "Little Flower," her "little way" of love, trust, and self-surrender, the Mass, the Cathedral—and now this dreadful careering down the hill. The memories were all there, fanned into a kind of pictorial vividness in the extraordinary clarity of my mind that night.

When my reflections had exhausted themselves I became aware of something like an interior voice, speaking in the inmost depths of my soul more powerfully and persuasively than my own reflections:

"You have been created out of nothing by the gratuitous love of God, who continues freely to preserve you in existence; otherwise you would return to nothingness. He has now come again to visit your soul. He has blessed you, regenerated you, and instructed you in the bosom of the true Church; He has preserved both your soul and body from innumerable dangers. You should thank Him with all your heart, since He has come to you, to tell you what He wills of you, for your desire to do all. Well may you be unhappy for the years you have lost. You deserve that

He should no longer speak to you, since you have so often been deaf to His voice, which called you to love Him, and so ungratefully turned your back upon Him."

"Enough, enough, my God!" I cried, "I know better than you that I am the chief of all sinners. Confucius had taught me early in my boyhood that 'one who gives offence to Heaven has nowhere else to expiate his sins.' By all reason, I should have been killed, or injured at least, in the forced landing of the plane, by the mortar shelling or this careering down the hill, but you spared me, as my grandmother did, when my sinful acts deserved severe punishment. Now tell me, in spite of my wretchedness, what is the remedy?"

Then the little interior voice continued:

"Tear off your Jekyll-Hyde mask! Here is His answer to your self-deceptions. You will find your end, not in yourself, in your self-love, in vanity, ambition, but in God. It is only through the sacrifice of your *whole* self to the cause of God that you can liberate yourself forever from the prison of a narrow and worldly egoism and taste the intense inner peace and purity of heart. It is a battle from beginning to end. Either go forward or come backward; either be a saint or a sinner. It is the Truth or falsehood. It is God or nothing. Neutrality in these great things is impossible. Nothing short of one hundred percent will do! Re-

211

member what Christ teaches you: 'Thou shalt love the Lord thy God with thy *whole* heart and with thy *whole* soul, and with *all* thy strength and with *all* thy mind.' "

Here is the clue-insight through which all the other insights may, in the end, be brought to their realization; the clue-insight without which all others are lost: *Stop asking what God will give you if you come to Him, and begin to ask what you will give God.* "What shall I render to the Lord," the Psalmist cries, "for all that he hath rendered to me? I will take the chalice of salvation, and I will call upon the name of the Lord."

I had no new vision that I can report, but I saw all. And now, after many vicissitudes, I handed myself over, body and soul. And now I was free: "Our soul hath been delivered as a sparrow out of the snare of the hunters. The snare is broken, and we are delivered" (Ps. 123: 7–8). Above all, I knew that there is only one happiness: to please Him; only one sorrow, to turn away from Him and to separate oneself from Him who is our life and all our joy. In having Him, I have everything besides. If my life belongs to Him and I place myself completely in His hands, what is the difference between homes, or jobs, or places, or times, or external conditions? The only thing that matters is coordination with the Truth, with the Reality which shapes all things and events according to God's will. As Dr. John C. H. Wu puts it: "With Christ, there is peace even in war. Without Christ, there is war even in peace. With Christ the poor are rich. Without Christ, the rich are poor. With Christ, adversity is sweet. Without Christ, prosperity is bitter. With Christ, the ignorant are wise. Without Christ, the wise are fools. With Christ, life is a prelude to Heaven. Without Christ, life is a prelude to Hell." *

Recently I came across this striking passage of St. John of the Cross in *The Dark Night,* and it seemed to me an exact description of how the soul advances by the light only of faith:

> "In this blissful night
> Secretly, no man seeing me,
> I seeing nothing,
> With no other light or guide
> But that which burned in my heart.
> And it led me
> Surer than the light of noonday."

God's grace is all. I was now ready for conversion, ready to grasp the reality of Our Lord's words: "You have not chosen Me, I have chosen you."

With divine grace, the rest was easy. A little meditation, a little more prayer; "My heart is ready." I was on my way. I had made my decision, the great and

---

* *Beyond East and West* (Sheed and Ward), p. 307.

final decision, though I still grasped at straws, seeking to hold myself back.

My two elder sons, George and Charles, returned to school in London, and I went back with my wife and youngest son to Rome. As soon as we arrived I called on Dr. Wu. Without telling him about the nearly tragic automobile accident and the crisis it had produced in my interior life, I straightforwardly brought my problem to him and asked simply if I could become a Catholic. He was only too pleased to hear this and recommended at once that I see Monsignor Stanislao Lokuang, who served as Ecclesiastical Counsellor of the Chinese Legation, to take instructions.

Early one morning when I got up from bed, I looked through the window and saw, on one of the rosebushes in the yard, a single long-stemmed rose of rare beauty. The bushes had been planted years ago but had never borne so much as a bud before now. I could not explain the case, except to interpret this flowering as a message from "The Little Flower," telling me that my holy marriage was near. And so it turned out. On the following day, the feast of St. Vincent Ferrer, I went on my knees together with my wife and youngest son in St. Agnes' Church in Rome.* It was April 5,

---

* Thanks be to God my eldest son, George, was baptized on the 8th of April, 1950 by Bishop Joseph M. Gilmore in St. Helena's Cathedral, Montana, and my second son

1949. All words are inadequate to express the peace
I had that day. I can only exclaim with the Psalmist:

> "The Lord is my shepherd:
>   I shall not want.
>   He makes me lie down in green pastures;
>   He leads me beside the refreshing waters.
>   He restores my soul."*

My act—done purely with the help of God—was a
nine days' wonder to my friends, but the fact is that,
after so many years of resisting the action of God
upon my life, in the manner I have related, I have at
last turned to look upon the full face of reality; recognized, at long last, what God is and what I am:
"God, infinite and eternal, Trinity, Unity; humanity,
finite, created in time, fallen, redeemed by Christ;
the individual man born into the life of nature, reborn into the life of grace, united with Christ in the
Church which is His Mystical Body, aided by angels,
hindered by devils, destined for heaven, in peril of
hell." † My entrance into the Church has meant only
the surrender of my will to what have long been the
dictates of logic for me.

Charles, and my baby-girl, Pauline, were baptized on the
26th of July, 1951 by Archbishop Paul Yu-pin in St. Mary
Magdalene's Church, New York.

* *The Psalms: A Prayer Book* (Benziger).

† F. J. Sheed, *Theology and Sanity*, p. 8.

So far as my wife is concerned, I am not in a position to penetrate her mind, but as one whose eyes have been fixed not on the immediate and often illusory objectives of material and social advancement, but on work, love and eternal truth, whose maturity has meant a constant spiritual growth, it seems a clear manifestation of the will of God that she should find fulfillment in living for Christ wherever she may find herself, under the sweet roof of the Church.

Obviously the story of my life up to the day of my baptism is hardly an adequate story of my "conversion." My conversion is still going on. As Father John T. S. Mao often told his Catholic friends: "The problem of how to live as a Christian is not solved by baptism alone." My baptism was not the end of my conversion but only the beginning—the orchestra tuning up, the curtain rising on the most important and absorbing drama in the world—man's search for the true light, for Christ, who is "the way, the truth, and the life," for *in lumine tuo lumen videbimus* (in Thy light we shall see light). It is a lifetime effort, every minute, every day, every year! As my dearest godfather, Dr. Wu, has often told me: "In the conversion of a soul, the grace of God is all, whereas human instruments are just like matchmakers who, after the wedding ceremony, withdraw from the scene and leave the bridegroom and his bride to themselves." In this sense I can do no more than to put in my heart the words of Blessed Nicholas of Flüe: "Lord, take from me everything that hinders me from going to Thee, give me all that will lead me to Thee, take me from myself and give me to Thyself," and to recite often the beautiful prayer of St. Francis of Assisi:

"Lord, make me an instrument of Thy peace.
Where there is hatred, let me sow love,
Where there is injury, let me sow pardon,
Where there is doubt, let me sow faith,
Where there is despair, let me sow hope,
Where there is darkness, let me sow light,
Where there is sadness, let me sow joy.
O Divine Master, grant that I may not so much seek
To be consoled as to console,
To be understood as to understand,
To be loved, as to love;
                    for
It is in giving that we receive,
It is in pardoning that we are pardoned,
It is in dying that we are born to eternal life."

EPILOGUE

Truth Is Universal

*"And of his fulness we all have
received: grace for grace. For
the law was given through
Moses; grace and truth came
through Jesus Christ"* (*John
1:16–17*).

G. K. Chesterton once said: "The Church is a house
with hundreds of gates, and no two men enter at
exactly the same angle." Indeed it is from a variety
of bypaths and over varied terrain that converts come
to the main highway leading to Damascus. This first
attempt to describe my religious pilgrimage would
make the scholarly Newman turn over in his grave.
It is very much like writing a book on China after
spending a week-end in Hongkong Repulse Bay. It
may be that those who have not made any kind of
study of Catholic philosophy will have difficulty in
discerning the logic of my course—although it is
equally possible that greater difficulty will be experienced by those who have! Furthermore, I do not
believe in people telling others of their faith, espe-

cially with a view to converting them. Faith does not permit telling; it must be lived, and then it is self-propagating; sanctity requires secrecy for its development.

However, my spiritual course must have some similarity to that of many souls in our modern world, and I am telling my story, not as an essay in theology, but as a record of personal experience in the pursuit of order, peace, and happiness; to a destination attained after many reverses on paths which started from widely distant points on the circumference of reality, and finally converged in the deep darkness over the central light of Truth. At least, so it seemed to me when, so often, I was plunged into incertitude, after I thought I had made a little progress. But as I look back I see that my progress was steadier than I thought at the time. I traversed a road sometimes in the blaze of sunlight, sometimes in midnight darkness; but never, I am convinced, without a Guide.

I cannot recall without tears of gratitude the day I was led to the true Light.* I approached the altar with an ineffable sense of peace, as I felt very clearly in

---

* I am especially grateful to Msgr. Stanislao Lokuang, who administered baptism to me on the 5th of April, 1949, to Archbishop Celso Còstantini, first Apostolic Delegate to China, who confirmed me sixteen days after my baptism, and to Abbot General D. Luigi Smith, who was my spiritual guide.

my heart that through no merit of my own the Good
Shepherd had made me rest in green pastures and
led me to the waters of refreshment. "By grace you
are saved through faith, and that not of yourselves, for
it is the gift of God" (Ephes. 2:8).

On the day of my baptism, the Holy Father, Pope
Pius XII, favored me, through Monsignor Montini,
with the apostolic benediction, which reads as follows:
*"Da Citta del Vaticano—Ai nuovi figli che regenerati
nei battesimo avvalorati dallo spirito nutriti della
divina Eucarestia entrano oggi nella Santa Milizia
Cristiana L'Augusto Pontefice invoca dal cielo fervore
di nuova vita nei Signore e imparte di cuore conforto
nell'ascesa la Sua prima paterna benedizione."* *

The following day the Holy Father granted me and
my family a special audience. We were privileged to
talk with His Holiness for about ten minutes. To this
moment I recall with deep gratitude the fatherly kind-
ness shown to us. I remember that the first time I
was received in a private audience was on the 10th
of November, 1945. As Chargé d'Affaires of the

---

* "From Vatican City
To the new sons who have been regenerated by baptism;
strengthened by the nourishing Spirit of the Divine Eucharist; who are entering today into the Holy Christian
Militia, His Holiness invokes from Heaven the fervour of
new life in Our Lord and imparts from his heart—with increasing spiritual joy—his first paternal benediction."

Chinese Embassy in Rome I, in the company of Dr. C. K. Sie, the first Chinese Minister to the Vatican, had the honor to present to His Holiness an autographed picture from President Chiang Kai-shek, with a personal letter in which the President expressed his great sense of gratitude to the Pope for his spiritual guidance and his encouragement of the Catholics in China, which had enabled them to stand bravely during the long years of the war with Japan.

Even a fleeting acquaintance with the Pope would have made a deep impression on me. A tall, thin man dressed in white, the Holy Father sat behind a long mahogany desk placed immediately at the right of the door, facing the rectangular, soberly furnished room. Instead of an aloof, cold or formally polite sovereign I found a completely unfettered, cordial and kindly Father who appeared engrossed in what I had to say. The quick intuition of his finely trained mind issued in a rapid-fire, question-and-answer dialogue, during which I perceived that His Holiness had fully understood my explanation and was already asking further questions. His Holiness has an amazing knack for going to the heart of a problem. I realize now how he acquires his immense, detailed information. This first conversation lasted more than half an hour and ended with a gift to me of a white rosary which the Holy Father had blessed. For nearly three years I carried the rosary in my overcoat pocket but hardly touched it. I do not know why.

When I went to Vatican City this second time, after baptism, I carried nothing with me but the white rosary. I knelt down and kissed His Holiness' ring and proceeded at once to pay him my respects in Italian. His reply to my address astonished me: he recalled what we had talked about at my first audience in 1945. After complimenting me on my Italian, he went on to say that China was the meeting point of East and West, and expressed the hope that the great task of conserving and deepening the ancient culture of China and giving it renewal through Christianity would be furthered by my entrance into the Church.

Although my conscience clearly revealed to me that I was only an unprofitable servant, the chief of all sinners who had brought the glorious Church of Christ nothing but my sins, I was so impressed and moved that I could not find words to make an appropriate reply, but could only say in my heart: "I have the rosary in my hand, and I will do the best I can."

But what role am I capable of playing in the immense task of re-evaluating Oriental culture in the light of Christianity? The role of a witness only; and so, in the hope that God's grace may supply what is wanting to me by nature, I have undertaken this work of describing my own spiritual odyssey, that it may perhaps be useful to others.

As I look back I realize that the fact that I was brought up as a Buddhist, learned to be a Confucianist, was educated in a Protestant school, and enlisted as an Oxford Groupist did not mean obstacles in my path, but rather incentives to me to accept the Catholic Church as the true Church of God.

Confucianism teaches people to "set the conscience right," and this is the starting point of a spiritual life. But Confucianism contains no means by which the spiritual life can develop. As Bishop Fulton Sheen says: "All human ideals, human codes, and human systems—whether Aristotelian, Confucian, Platonic— treat man as a self-contained being whose highest potentialities exist within his own nature. But the pressure of the Eternal on his soul incites the Christian to become something he is not—entices him to permit himself to be lifted to a higher level than the human alone can ever possibly attain. That is why the initiative must come from God, as he works within us." * I was feeling this "pressure of the Eternal" when I turned to Christianity.

Protestantism affords an incentive to embrace the ideology of universal love; MRA further advances this

---

* *Lift Up Your Heart* (Whittlesey), p. 199.

226

principle, puts the belief into more practical order. But the weakness in Protestantism and MRA alike is that neither realizes the help which God has ordained shall be received through the Sacraments; as one tries to practise Protestantism and fails, one experiences the need of the sacramental nourishment afforded by a full Catholic life.

It is impossible to describe in words the vital reality of life in the Church, nourished by the sacraments; their function is realized only through the slow growth of experience. But even an observer from outside the Church cannot fail to perceive their wonderful conformity to the pattern of human development. As Father John Arintero puts it, in his book *The Mystical Evolution in the Development and Vitality of the Church:*

For each of the principal functions of the Christian life, both private and collective, there is a sacrament. We are reborn through baptism; we are nourished and we grow through the Eucharist; we are strengthened by the character of virility and become soldiers of Christ through confirmation; our spiritual infirmities are cured, and we even recover life anew through penance; we purge the remnants of evil which penance did not erase, and we dispose ourselves to appear before the Supreme Judge by means of extreme unction. By holy orders spiritual government is provided as well as the continued dispensing of the divine mysteries, and by matrimony there is provided the sanctified propagation of Christian people.*

In the great doctrine of the Mystical Body I find the answers to my groping after the mysterious connection between suffering and love. There is indeed no living in love without suffering; but in the Church there is no isolated individual, all live in the life of the Body and the merit that each soul gains through suffering in a Christian way is communicated to the whole Body. Not only this, but the life of the Body, sustained by suffering in Christ, is communicated to the whole world, and the Church is the joy of the world: "You shall draw waters with joy out of the saviour's fountains" (Is. 12:3).

I have already pointed out, in the course of this book, how through the reading of Dante I became reintegrated with the Chinese tradition. This was the beginning of the process of intellectual liberation which I have experienced in entering the Church. Nothing can be thought or done in this world outside the Providence of God, who holds all things in being. The mind of the Catholic, enlightened by universal truth, can draw forth the wisdom of the great pagan thinkers without being bound by their limitations, gain new insights from the great Protestant divines without

---

* (Herder, 1949).

being misled by their errors—in fact, benefit from them to the extent to which, even though they did not have the whole truth, they contributed to human history a certain increase and growth. Thus I am glad to be Buddha's debtor in the matter of ascetical purification, Confucius' in that of a lofty ideal of moral perfection, Laotse's in that of tolerance and detachment, Luther's in that of non-conformism, and for these things I honor them; they are still alive for me.

Since I have become a Catholic, I have found that nothing of the Chinese tradition is lost to me, but on the contrary I have brought forth new treasures from old. The truth of the matter is that it would be far more difficult to reconcile Confucius with paganism than with Christ, and it is through Christianity that Confucius is illuminated for me. Through the peculiar circumstances of my own life, in which the traditions of East and West are united, I have come to realize the implications of the fact that truth is universal. Otto Karrer analyzes the matter very clearly on theological grounds:

If the westerner represents the reasoning and active, the oriental the passive and mystical type of humanity, neither can claim the sanction of Christian principles for his attitude as against the other. On the contrary, the dogmatic theology of Catholic Christianity supports the ideal mean between these two types of thought and experience. And it is no accident that the greatest Christians and the great Apostles of Christianity have always felt the attraction of this spiritual bridge, of a sublime synthesis of East and West, a vital interchange between both spiritual hemispheres. And this means, not the rejection of either component, but their organic union.*

But in order to give any real hint of the fullness of truth that I find in Catholic life, I must turn to poetry and let Mother Church herself speak, through the words of Gertrud von Le Fort:

"In my arms I still carry flowers from the wilderness, the dew on my hair is from the valleys of the dawn of mankind.

I have prayers that the meadows lend an ear to, I know how storms are tempered, how water is blest.

I carry in my womb the secrets of the desert, on my head the noble web of ancient thought.

For I am mother to all Earth's children: why do you scorn me, world, when my Heavenly Father makes me so great?

Behold, in me long-vanished generations still kneel, and out of my soul many pagans shine toward the infinite.

I lay hidden in the temples of their gods, I was darkly present in the sayings of their wise men.

---

* *The Religions of Mankind* (Sheed and Ward), p. 211.

I was on the towers with their star-gazers, I was with
      the solitary women on whom the spirit de-
      scended.
I was the desire of all times, I was the light of all
      times, I am the fullness of all times.
I am their great union, I am their eternal oneness.
I am the way of all their ways, on me the millennia
      are drawn to God."*

How immeasurable is my debt to Mother Church
for making all things new! Since I have been reborn
in Christ, the wisdom of China has yielded its rich-
ness in truth, what has been partial is becoming full,
the things that were wanting to me have been supplied,
never to be lost again.

---

* From *Hymns to the Church*, translated by Margaret
Chanler (Sheed and Ward).